DONCASTER'S RAILWAY LEGENDS

Written, photographed, compiled
and edited by Brian Sharpe
Design: Fran Lovely
Sub Editors: Sarah Lawson and Val Dawson
Publisher: Dan Savage

Additional contributions and
photographs supplied with grateful thanks by:
Gavin Morrison, David Hopper, John Crawley,
Maurice Burns and Colour-Rail.

Published by
Mortons Media Group Ltd
Media Centre, Morton Way,
Horncastle, Lincolnshire LN9 6JR
Tel: 01507 523456.

Printed by
William Gibbons and Son, Wolverhampton

Published August 2007

Doncaster's Railway
LEGENDS

There is a proud history of locomotive building in the town of Doncaster and this book is a tribute to the famous locomotives built there and the men who built, maintained and operated them.

Known as Danum in Roman times, and Dona Ceastra (camp on the Don) by the Saxons, Doncaster's first documented resident, the Praefectus equitum Crispianorum was a Roman military leader stationed in Doncaster at the turn of the fifth century AD. His unit was originally raised from tribespeople living near the town of Crispiana in Upper Pannonia, near Zirc in the Bakony region of western Hungary. That such a force should be stationed at Doncaster shows the cosmopolitan nature of Roman Britain. The unit formed part of the forces under the command of Dux Britanniarum or the 'Duke of the Britons', commander of Roman forces along the northern border of the empire.

The fact that this is known, shows the importance of Doncaster, even to the Romans, as records were kept and have survived.

In more recent times, among Doncaster's best-known contemporary residents is Lesley Garrett. Lesley was born on 10 April 1955 in Thorne, Doncaster. She studied music to A-level before training for six years at the Royal Academy of Music. Both of her grandfathers were musical, one was a classical pianist.

Doncaster has always been an important transport hub. Ancient trackways converged at the point where the river Don first became fordable. Later the Romans chose the same point to cross the river, building a number of important roads and ridgeways in the area. The north-south route developed into the Great North Road linking London with the north and Scotland. The Don was also improved for navigation allowing Humber Keels to travel far inland thus making the town an important inland port.

Doncaster was to make a contribution to Britain's development totally disproportionate to its size and status. The coming of the railways transformed Britain, and many hitherto small settlements grew into major conurbations as a result of their railway-related industries. Crewe, Swindon and Doncaster; these are just three towns which will forever be regarded as 'railway towns' but Doncaster has a unique claim to fame. It took the art of railway engineering to new heights. Only one railway workshop is responsible for producing the steam engine that went faster than any other in the world, and it was Doncaster.

It was not an isolated occurrence, 'The Plant' as Doncaster's locomotive-building workshop became known, had been at the forefront of the quest for power, economy, efficiency, and speed for many years, and while the record-breaking *Mallard* may have been the fastest-ever, there were many other spectacular achievements by Doncaster-built machines over the years leading up to its world record achievement in 1938.

Rail is not the only method of transport, but in the days of steam at least, it was the only method which relied on the sweat and toil of human endeavour not only to build the engines to the finest-possible quality, but to get the best out of them in daily service. A steam engine is an individual, it performs differently each day. An aircraft or a car lacks the individuality of a steam engine, only a ship can perhaps compare, but on a totally different scale.

It was the combination of the skill and expertise built up over many years at Doncaster, plus the hard work and determination of the men working the engines, inspired by the leadership of railway management, which produced the team effort required to make that world speed record in 1938, a record which still stands.

Where did Doncaster really stand in a hypothetical league table of Britain's great railway workshops? To answer that question, we need to establish what sets one apart from another; it is not just about size or longevity, but about making the most significant contributions to advancing the technology of the day.

Crewe was a busier and more important station, and is better known as a railway junction than Doncaster. Although the latter built some of Britain's fastest and most famous steam engines, such as *Flying Scotsman* and *Mallard*, a surprisingly small proportion now survive, and two of the streamlined Pacifics are in America. Surprisingly, 'The Plant' built hardly any diesels apart from shunters until the late 1970s.

Doncaster works only really had three significant chiefs during its heyday of steam locomotive construction, Stirling, Ivatt and particularly the third, Herbert Nigel (later Sir Nigel) Gresley. Of the others, Thompson had to contend with wartime conditions and Peppercorn's reign was brief as Nationalisation took hold. Gresley undoubtedly produced among the top steam locomotive designs during steam's finest hour, but how did these designs compare with contemporary design elsewhere? ■

The most famous of all of Doncaster's products; LNER A3 Pacific No 60103 *Flying Scotsman* **receives an overhaul to prepare it for a further period of hard work hauling East Coast Main Line expresses, inside 'The Plant' on 20 March 1960.** GAVIN MORRISON

The railway comes to Doncaster

Transport has played an important role in Doncaster's heritage. The stagecoach trade of the 17th and 18th centuries generated the wealth that built the town centre in the Georgian fashion complete with one of only three Mansion Houses in Britain as its civic headquarters. Horse breeding for the stagecoach trade gave rise to Doncaster Racecourse, one of the best known in Britain, and home to the St Leger.

The Great Northern Railway built its principal route from King's Cross to York, which was to become the southern part of the East Coast Main Line. Originally, trains ran via east Lincolnshire, turning north-east at Peterborough, to Boston, then to Lincoln, and Gainsborough. They then turned to the south-west on to the Manchester Sheffield & Lincolnshire Railway to Retford, before regaining a northerly route through Doncaster, to Askern Junction, where the GNR originally made an end-on connection with the Lancashire & Yorkshire Railway. GNR trains then took another devious route via Knottingley over the L&Y to join the arch-enemy York & North Midland Railway to reach York, or alternatively to run over the North Midland Railway to Leeds.

The L&Y ran the first passenger trains into the GNR's Doncaster station, from West Yorkshire on 8 September 1848 just in time for it to carry no less than 30,000 passengers per day during St Leger week!

The GNR started its King's Cross to York service via Doncaster in 1850 by the roundabout route through Boston, Doncaster and Knottingley, and although it quickly shortened its route from London to Doncaster, the North Eastern Railway did not build its more direct route from York via Selby to Shaftholme Junction, until as late as 1871.

The Manchester Sheffield & Lincolnshire Railway built a more direct route between Lincoln and Retford in 1850, which the GNR was able to use until it completed its far-shorter and originally-planned 'Towns Line' from Peterborough to Retford via Grantham and Newark, in 1852.

At the same time as the GNR had reached Doncaster, the South Yorkshire Railway also reached the town from Swinton, running to a triangular junction with the GNR at Bridge Junction just south of the present station. It built its own station at Cherry Tree Lane, but this was shortlived and in

An East Coast Main Line express approaches Doncaster from the north in February 2007. The line to Scunthorpe and Cleethorpes swings round to the right, while the Leeds line diverges to the north-west behind the train. BRIAN SHARPE

1850, both this and the original GNR station at Marshgate closed and a new station was opened on the site of the present station.

Initially, the GNR ran the passenger trains on the SYR, and the hated Midland Railway ran the goods trains. The SYR was leased by the Manchester Sheffield & Lincolnshire Railway from 1861 and taken over in 1864, becoming part of the main line from Sheffield to Doncaster.

Doncaster's railway map remained remarkably static for more than 15 years, until two independent companies built the other main lines which now radiate from the town. The South Yorkshire Railway & River Dun Navigation Company (as the SYR had become) had built a meandering line from Marshgate towards Scunthorpe following the river, which lasted only until 1866 when the MSLR completed a more modern alignment from Doncaster station to Scunthorpe and South Humberside. This of course gave that company a route from Manchester via Doncaster to South Humberside, an important part of the present-day railway map.

The GNR acquired significant routes in the Leeds/Bradford area, which remained isolated, and so was keen to open its own routes from Doncaster to Leeds and York, but was continually frustrated. In 1866, the West Riding & Grimsby Railway, built the line from Wakefield to Stainforth, designed to give the MSLR access to Hull, plus a branch into Doncaster, and this company was quickly acquired by the Great Northern and the Manchester Sheffield & Lincolnshire jointly.

The WR&G had built the line across from Adwick to join the MSLR at Stainforth & Hatfield, crossing the GN's main line to the north, immediately south of Askern Junction where the GN and L&Y met. The WR&GR gave the GNR its route to Leeds.

The GNR also built a shorter route from Gainsborough into Doncaster in 1867, but this never formed part of the ECML, in fact from 1879 it was transferred into joint ownership with the Great Eastern Railway, partly to stop the GER joining with the L&Y to bypass Doncaster completely and threaten the GNR's domination.

When the NER built its route from Selby to Shaftholme Junction in 1871, this completed Doncaster's railway system as far as long-term passenger routes were concerned, but railway building was to restart in earnest 40 years later. ∎

Below: Great Northern Railway Ivatt small Atlantic No 252 at Doncaster on 31 January 1913.

Great Northern Railway

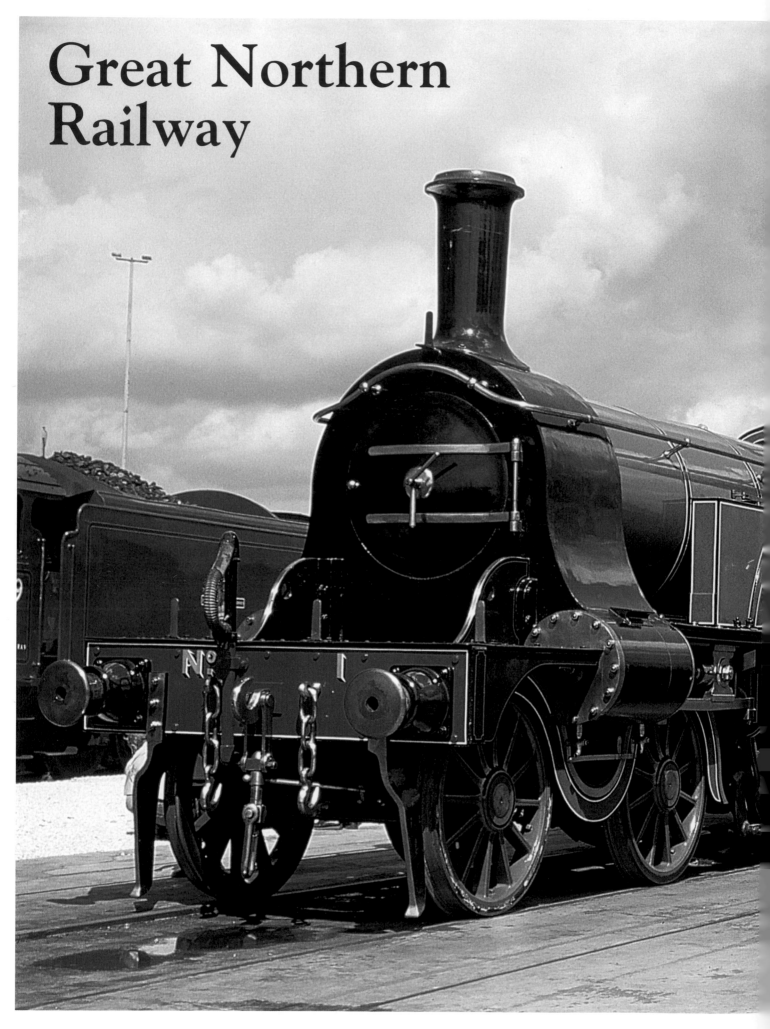

Britain's first north-south railways bypassed Doncaster, though not by much. Had this continued the town could easily have become a quiet backwater. Doncastrian, and MP for the West Riding of Yorkshire, Sir Edmund Beckett Denison was not going to let this happen however. Through his influence as chairman of the Great Northern Railway Company he ensured Doncaster was placed firmly on the railway map.

There had been a plan for the GNR to run from Gainsborough to Selby, well to the east of Doncaster, but Denison insisted on what became known as the 'towns line', which included Doncaster. In the end the GNR pressed on with two routes to the north, one via Boston, with a branch to Grimsby, and one via Newark. The company had difficulty in obtaining consent for building all of the planned sections, and this was eventually to lead to direct lines being built from Retford, and from Gainsborough, joining just south of Doncaster, and for the GNR to reach only as far as Askern, a few miles north of Doncaster.

The GNR grew to encompass the originally planned main lines from King's Cross to Doncaster, and to Grimsby. It also served Cambridge, Lincoln and Nottingham, with a branch continuing to Derby, plus Leicester and Stafford through joint line arrangements. Through acquisitions of smaller companies, it became an important player in the West Riding though, with a main line running from Doncaster to Leeds and Bradford, plus a network of branches in the Leeds, Bradford area. The section of main line between Doncaster and Wakefield was owned jointly with the Great Central Railway, while the Doncaster-Lincoln-Cambridge line was owned jointly with the Great Eastern Railway.

Apart from its main lines to the north, it was not a particularly extensive system, and a very large part of its network in Lincolnshire closed in 1970 leaving the east of the county almost bereft of railways; just the meandering branch from Grantham through Sleaford and Boston to Skegness remaining. ∎

Stirling Single No1 at Doncaster works with classic GNR and ECJS teak coaches during the 2003 150th anniversary celebrations.
ROBIN JONES

East Coast Main Line

We all know the East Coast Main Line (ECML) as one of Britain's premier rail routes, promoted as the 'Route of the Flying Scotsman' by present operators Great North Eastern Railway (GNER).

The route was built in a piecemeal fashion during the years of 'Railway Mania'. The GNR promoted the London (King's Cross) to York section, the North Eastern Railway that grew out of the York & North Midland and other railways, ended up with the Shaftholme Junction to Berwick-upon-Tweed section in the middle, and the North British Railway, the Scottish portion, from Berwick to Edinburgh and beyond.

Edinburgh is widely regarded as the northern end of the ECML, but expresses have always continued further, although once over the Forth and Tay bridges, and past Dundee, important sections were owned by the Caledonian Railway, and therefore in terms of ownership, more properly regarded as part of the West Coast Main Line.

The first railway to connect London with York had effectively been built by companies which later became part of the Midland Railway and the North Eastern Railway, and were built to serve as many centres of population, industry and commerce as possible, as opposed to linking two distant cities by the shortest possible route. Therefore, Doncaster lost out, as the main route to the north was a little further west and linked Sheffield and York. In fact York was not a large place, nor did it have significant heavy industry, but it was an important regional centre; George Hudson, the 'Railway King' made it his 'capital' and it became an important railway centre, its station being the largest in the world when it was built.

Once the GNR set its sights on reaching York though, the scene was set for a high-speed railway route from London to the north, straight and level, across easy flat terrain for much of the way. By the time the GNR had reached Doncaster from London, and the NER joined it from York, the route already continued to Darlington and Newcastle, and courtesy of the North British, right into the Scottish capital.

The through express service was inaugurated from King's Cross to Edinburgh, in 1864; the most important train, the 10am departure from King's Cross soon becoming known (to the public at least) as the 'Flying Scotsman'.

To most long-distance passengers, Doncaster was little more than the last stop on the Great Northern before trains joined North Eastern metals, in fact on some expresses it was not even a stop! History though

One of the engines which became synonymous with the East Coast Main Line in steam days; Doncaster-built Gresley A4 streamlined Pacific No 60017 *Silver Fox* leaves Doncaster with an up express. GAVIN MORRISON

would see Doncaster play an unequalled role in shaping the future of what was to be one of the most important rail routes in Britain.

Until 1923, King's Cross to Edinburgh expresses would continue to run over the tracks of three separate railway companies. But even at an early stage, Doncaster's influence would start to be felt well beyond the theoretical boundary of the GNR at Shaftholme Junction, just a few miles north of Doncaster. ■

A Virgin Voyager unit on a north-east – south-west service speeds past Shaftholme Junction, where until 1870, the GNR's expresses originally turned to the left on to the Lancashire & Yorkshire Railway to reach York via Knottingley.
BRIAN SHARPE

EWS Class 66 No 66155 takes the LYR line towards Knottingley at Shaftholme Junction with the daily Middleton Towers (Norfolk) to Monk Bretton (Barnsley) sand train.
BRIAN SHARPE

Above: LNER A1 Pacific No 60131 *Osprey* pauses with an up express at Retford as No 60144 *Kings Courier* slows for the station with a down express in the summer of 1959. DAVID HOPPER

The 'Towns Line'

The GNR set out to build a main line from London to York, as well as to east Lincolnshire.

Initially, having reached Peterborough, the line swung north-east to run dead straight to Boston, then while a line turned north across the Wolds to Grimsby, the original route to York diverged from this line just north of Boston and ran through Tattershall and Bardney to Lincoln, then to Gainsborough. From Gainsborough, trains ran via Retford to eventually reach Doncaster.

The direct route from Peterborough to Doncaster through Grantham, Newark and Retford did not open until 1852. ∎

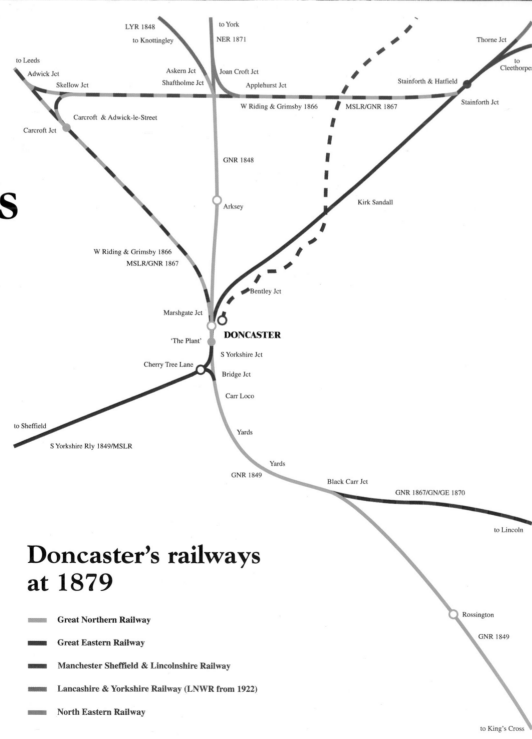

Doncaster's railways at 1879

Great Northern Railway

Great Eastern Railway

Manchester Sheffield & Lincolnshire Railway

Lancashire & Yorkshire Railway (LNWR from 1922)

North Eastern Railway

Class 47 No 47426 heads south out of Doncaster towards Retford at Black Carr Junction on 4 September 1976. Black Carr was the meeting point of the GNR lines from Gainsborough and Retford into Doncaster. By 1920, this once straightforward junction had grown into one of the most complex series of railway junctions outside London. Much of the old railway infrastructure survived the changeover from steam to diesel traction, but has since been swept away by electrification. BRIAN SHARPE

Boston

Doncaster's predecessor

The GNR did not commence locomotive building until 1867, a full 20 years after it had inaugurated its express services from King's Cross to the north. In the early days of railways, many companies bought their locomotives from private contractors, and some continued to do so. Even the GNR sub-contracted a considerable amount of locomotive production throughout its existence, but like all of the major railway companies, it preferred to build its own once it had the capability. The GNR's first locomotive and carriage repair works were at Boston in Lincolnshire, not a town usually noted for locomotive building.

Some of these buildings, which were the GNR's first repair workshops from 1848, can still be seen near Bridge Street level crossing by the station.

In 1850, Archibald Sturrock was appointed as locomotive engineer for the GNR and as the company's expansion plans looked likely to outgrow its small facilities at Boston, thought was given to building much more extensive premises.

But the choice of Sturrock and the majority of the Board was the central location of Peterborough.

Again Denison had to argue and lobby to get Doncaster given the recognition it deserved, but he had a fight on his hands, and it was not until 1851 that his arguments won the day, and by 1853, all the company's heavy locomotive work was moved to Doncaster. It was to be another 14 years though before a locomotive was actually built there. ■

The GNR's buildings at Boston now play a role in keeping the town's citizens fit and healthy. BRIAN SHARPE

Archibald Sturrock,

rchibald Sturrock was a Scot, born in Angus. He was trained at various engineering works in Dundee, and had railway experience in a variety of gauges, including a short spell as works manager for the GWR at Swindon under Daniel Gooch in broad gauge days, and came to the GNR with Isambard Brunel's personal recommendation.

Edmund Bury was first locomotive engineer of the GNR but was not felt suited to the company once the main line was built, partly as he remained a senior partner of his locomotive building firm in Liverpool.

When the job was advertised, 31 applications were received, and one of the youngest applicants, Archibald Sturrock, 34, with his letter of recommendation from no less than IK Brunel, was recruited from the GWR, commencing his employment on 27 March 1850.

Despite having favoured the Peterborough option for the location of

the GNR's new workshops, Sturrock was effectively based at Doncaster from 24 July 1852. By December of that year, 949 men were employed at Doncaster works, 700 having transferred from Boston.

A great believer in a large, easy-to-fire, free-steaming boilers, Sturrock soon started to design his own engines, rather than simply buy the contractors' own designs, but the construction was still left to the contractor.

Sturrock's locomotive designs, which were inevitably based to an extent on Swindon thinking, were ahead of their time, and Sturrock was looking for increased speed and power from his express locomotives, to enable them to compete effectively for Anglo-Scottish passenger traffic.

He was given almost a blank chequebook by the GNR directors to make its operations as efficient as possible. He immediately designed

locomotive superintendent of the GNR

engines with boiler pressures of 150psi, more than 50 per cent up on existing types both on the GNR and elsewhere.

Sturrock inherited 150 engines in 1851 and by 1866, 282 more had been built to his designs. Many were goods engines, but he will be remembered for his 2-2-2 and 2-4-0 express engines.

For an increased salary, Sturrock had also taken on the role of carriage and wagon superintendent as well. His coaches were the best on the East Coast route, and used almost exclusively on Anglo-Scottish expresses, and uniquely, the GNR moved its coal traffic in its own wagons.

He even went as far as building a 4-2-2, intended to run from King's Cross to Edinburgh throughout in eight hours. No 215 never achieved this, and was never really much use, having had to be rebuilt from its original 2-2-2-2 configuration to try to get it to stay on the track at all. But Sturrock claimed it would do 75mph, and his idea proved to be

years ahead of its time.

The GNR had flimsy rails, and Sturrock addressed this by designing steam tenders for his goods engines. This was a way of obtaining more power without producing a heavier engine. However these engines were not so successful, and were unpopular with the crews, who had twice as much work to do, while being permanently enveloped in steam. The unreliability of these engines undoubtedly led to Sturrock's premature departure, although whether he jumped or was pushed is open to question.

Always a healthy sportsman, he married into great wealth at the age of 50, and walked away from engineering and railways completely. He assumed the role of an English country squire. Nevertheless, by the time of Sturrock's departure in 1866, the GNR had 460 steam engines, though still none actually built by the company. ■

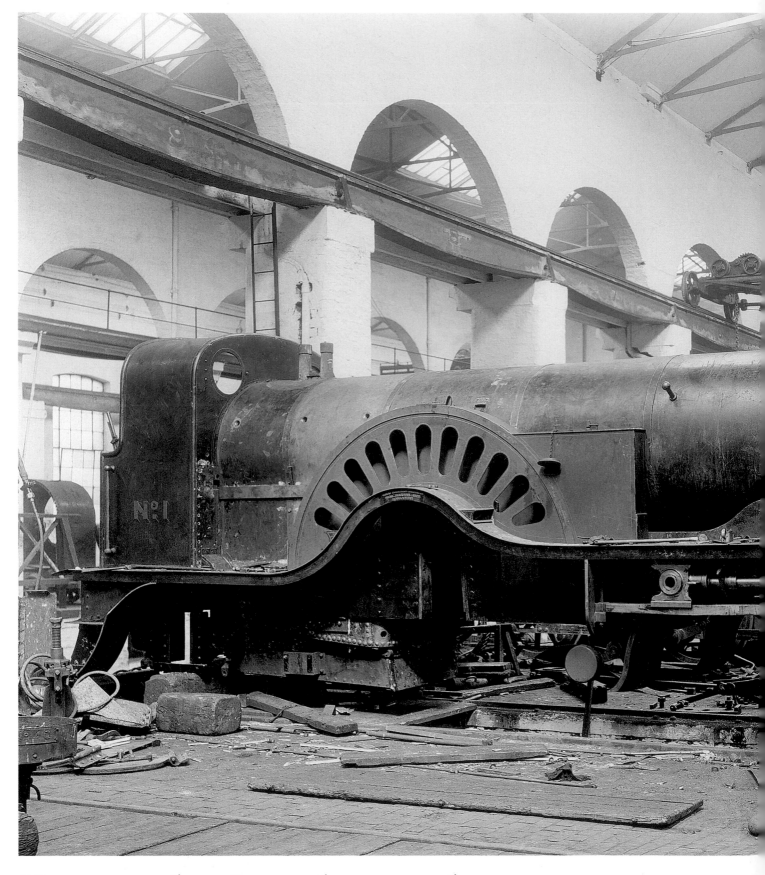

Patrick Stirling, locomotive superintendent of the GNR

Locomotive Works in Glasgow. He was then appointed in 1851 to be superintendent of a short line between Bowling on the River Clyde and Balloch on Loch Lomond, which later became a part of the North British Railway. In 1853 he was appointed to the position of locomotive superintendent of the Glasgow & South Western Railway (GSWR).

In 1866, after 13 years at the GSWR, Stirling moved to the Great Northern Railway at Doncaster where he stayed until dying in office in 1895. During the early years of Stirling's tenure, many new engines were required for the new routes, which were still being built.

In April 1867, Stirling obtained approval to build three 0-4-2s at Doncaster. No 18 was the first of 709 engines built at 'The Plant' to Stirling's designs.

Stirling built his engines for speed and power, in order to handle some of the continuous gradients on the GNR's main line to York, and to compete against the Midland Railway and LNWR in the Races to the North. A product of this particularly competitive era in railway history was the famous Stirling Singles. These were elegant 4-2-2s with 8ft driving wheels, and domeless boilers.

None of the Singles survived into regular LNER stock, although No.1 is now a part of the National Collection at the National Railway Museum in York.

Stirling was a strict Scots patriarch of formal habits and sober tastes, all in the Presbyterian manner, and with a large family of daughters. He had moved to the GNR after being locomotive superintendent of the Glasgow & South Western Railway; a position his brother James also once held on the GSWR. James Stirling was also at one time locomotive engineer of the South Eastern Railway. Patrick's son Matthew was a long-serving locomotive engineer of the Hull & Barnsley Railway.

Stirling was well liked by the railwaymen of the GNR. For his 70th birthday, they erected a fountain in his honour in Doncaster. When he died in office on 11 November 1895 at the age of 76, 3000 GNR railwaymen braved pouring rain to accompany his funeral procession.

The Patrick Stirling memorial lamp and fountain where originally located in St Sepulchregate near the railway station. It was then moved to St James Bridge and finally to Patrick Stirling Court in 1993 where it can be seen to this day. The inscription reads: 'This fountain was presented to the town of Doncaster by the enginemen and firemen employed on The Great Northern Railway, in commemoration of the 70th birthday of P Stirling, Esq CE locomotive engineer to the company. To mark the respect and esteem in which he is held by them June 29th 1890.

Opened by Mrs Stirling August 11th J.F.Clark, Esq. mayor'.

An imprinted representation of a Stirling Single can be seen on the parapet of the footbridge across Balby Road near St James' Church, Doncaster. ∎

Stirling 8ft Single No 1 in 'The Plant' at Doncaster. In fact the engine is not under construction, but 18 years after withdrawal from service, has just been fitted with a new boiler so that it could appear in steam at the Stockton & Darlington Centenary Cavalcade in 1925.

Patrick Stirling was another Scot, in fact the cousin of his predecessor Archibald Sturrock. Born in Kilmarnock in 1820, his father, the Reverend Robert Stirling was the ingenious inventor of the Hot Air or Stirling Cycle Engine. Stirling began his engineering career as an apprentice in his uncle's Stirling Foundry in Dundee. He worked his way up to become erecting shop foreman at Neilson's

Stirling's Singles

The transformation of Doncaster's workshops from repair and maintenance only, to design and construction as well, was overseen by Patrick Stirling who became the GNR's locomotive superintendent in 1866. He introduced the revolutionary Stirling Singles, transforming the GNR's express services, and firmly established 'The Plant' at the forefront of world transport technology and design.

Wheel arrangement is an important factor in determining a steam locomotive's performance. Right from an early stage, the Stockton & Darlington Railway's *Locomotion* had four small driving wheels, making it suitable for goods traffic, while Stephenson's *Rocket* was an 0-2-2 with only two driving wheels, but they were big, to provide speed rather than power.

As steam engines developed, four-coupled designs predominated for goods trains, or passenger trains on demanding routes, while single-wheelers were favoured for light expresses. Most railways in the mid-19th century used little other than 2-2-2s for express services.

While Stirling's 4-2-2s now look ancient, they were a tremendous step forward, able to accommodate a larger boiler and able to sustain power output for much longer than earlier designs. Some of the design detail can be seen to have influenced later generations of engineers at Doncaster for more than 50 years.

The noted railway historian, Derek Cross wrote about the Stirling Singles, they "have perhaps received more publicity than was earned by their performance in the 1895 race to Aberdeen." Yet equally respected railway historian OS Nock states in his book *The Great Northern Railway* "No locomotive class caught and fired the imagination of the travelling public more than Patrick Stirling's 8ft bogie Singles." and "The performance of the Singles grew to be almost a legend in itself. The eight-footers did some of their finest work in the Aberdeen races."

The history of GNR locomotive design is clearly a matter of opinion, and experts cannot agree. Perhaps the Stirling Singles were a victim of their own success. They were good enough to actually lead to an increase in traffic to levels they simply could not cope with.

But the 45, later 53 engines, hauled Britain's, therefore the world's fastest trains.

Stirling corresponded with David Joy about fitting a version of Joy's valve gear to his Single, but eventually was not prepared to allow the appearance of his engine to be spoilt. There were some serious accidents though, and although engines and their designers were exonerated, GNR express train operation and the strains put on engines, track and footplate crews, were called into question.

Archibald Sturrock had built a 4-2-2, but his express designs had been 2-2-2s. When Stirling took over, he initially designed and built 2-2-2s and these remained in front-line service for many years. It was the development of these into Stirling's 4-2-2 design, producing 25 per cent more tractive effort than the earlier engines, with its much longer boiler, larger driving wheel, and steadier ride at high speed, which enabled the GNR to really accelerate its expresses. It

is the 4-2-2s which are remembered as Stirling's Singles, although the description applies equally to the smaller 2-2-2s.

In the 1870s and 1880s, the GNR was unusual among British railways in not being ashamed of claiming that its expresses ran fast, although its published working timetables were still compiled on the basis of a theoretical maximum speed of 60mph.

Contemporary accounts of the performance of Stirling's Singles on the 'Flying Scotsman' in the 1888 'Race to the North' showed both 7ft 7in 2-2-2s and 8ft 4-2-2s averaging between 55 and 59mph between King's Cross and Grantham, and Grantham and York, with around 100-ton trains, the fastest being a 2-2-2 which reached Grantham (105.5 miles) in 105 minutes from King's Cross. ∎

Stirling's Singles were relegated to secondary duties later in their lives. A1 No 1004 waits to leave Boston with the 3.30pm train to Lincoln in 1913, shortly before withdrawal during the following year.
FH GILLFORD, JOHN CRAWLEY COLLECTION

Above: The GNR engine repair shops at Doncaster.

'The Plant':
Doncaster Works

In 1853, the GNR established an 11-acre site on the edge of Doncaster for the repair and maintenance of locomotives and carriages, replacing earlier facilities at Boston and Peterborough. From these beginnings, the railway works known locally, and throughout the railway industry, as 'The Plant' grew.

The building south of the footbridge is the oldest part of the works (called Denison House). Behind is the original erecting shop with space for 30 engines. Locomotives entered the works from the south, carriages and wagons from the north.

A new erecting shop was built in 1891, further west. In 1889, wagon building and repair was relocated to the Carr, south of Doncaster, near the locomotive running sheds.

Stirling felt that locomotive repair was inadequate and too much heavy work was being

Right: GNR J50 0-6-0T Departmental No 11 is ex-works at Doncaster and ready for further action as works shunter in January 1964.
COLOUR-RAIL BRE 2039

(Map labels:) STRIPPING SHOP, TUBE REPAIR SHOP, WHEEL SHOP, CRIMPSALL ERECTING SHOP, KIRK ST, CANTEEN, LOCOMOTIVE PAINT SHOP, ELECTRIC POWER HOUSE, AMBULANCE ROOM, IRON FOUNDRY, PATTERN SHOP, BOILER SHOP, FORGE, NEW ERECTING SHOP, TIN SHOP, RIVER DON, WEST CARRIAGE SHOP, STORES, OFFICES, BRASS FOUNDRY, ELECTRIC DEPT, SPRING SHOP, FABRICATION SHOP, TIMBER STACK, TIMBER DRYING SHED, STORE, BATTERY SHOP, GRINDING SHOP, WHITE METAL, M/C FITTERS SHOP, LIGHT MACHINE SHOP, SMITHS SHOP, CARRIAGE PAINT SHOP, CARRIAGE BUILDING SHOP, TRAIN ELECTRICIANS, MAIN MACHINE SHOP, TRIMMERS SHOP, BRIDGE TERRACE, HEXTHORPE ROAD, OFFICE, CENTRAL DRAWING OFFICE, C.M.E.'s OFFICE, NORTH CARRIAGE CGE. BRASS SHOP, NORTH CARRIAGE SHED, PASSENGER STATION, NORTH BRIDGE

farmed out to local depots. A new locomotive repair shop was established in an area known as Crimpsall, to the west of the site, able to accommodate 100 engines.

The works developed and expanded with the rising fortunes of GNR. Like the other major railway companies, the GNR wished to establish its own locomotive design and construction facilities. From 1867 therefore 'The Plant' added locomotive manufacturing to its existing role when, in April 1867, Stirling obtained approval to build three 0-4-2s at Doncaster. No 18 was the first of 709 engines built at 'The Plant' to Stirling's designs.

No one could have foreseen then just how significant a contribution this establishment would make to the history of train travel in Britain. ∎

LNER A3 Pacific No 60037 *Hyperion* ex-works at Doncaster paint shop in May 1962.
COLOUR-RAIL BRE 1835

HA Ivatt, locomotive superintendent of the GNR

I n 1879, the GNR introduced the first dining car, and from 1893, this luxury became available to third as well as first class passengers. Amenity, not speed, became the order of the day. Coaches got much bigger, and trains of course, became heavier.

The MSLR's London extension to Marylebone threatened the GNR, but by some horse trading, the GNR retained its King's Cross–Manchester expresses, now running via Nottingham with GNR engines throughout. With GNR goods workings over the Pennines similarly expanded, Doncaster had to come up with another 70 engines at the turn of the century, not all of which could be home produced.

Patrick Stirling's successor was Henry Alfred Ivatt, who was trained on the LNWR at Crewe and had later held the position of district locomotive superintendent of the Southern District of the Great Southern & Western Railway at Cork in Ireland. Ivatt walked the entire 156 miles of the Great Northern main line after his appointment and was appalled at the state of the track.

Ivatt realised that for express trains, what was needed now was not bigger wheels and faster running, but greater boiler power. His first engines, some 2-4-0s, could not carry large enough boilers. His first express engines were 4-4-0s carrying some of the biggest boilers in Britain, but still not big enough. Ivatt extended the frames and added a pair of carrying wheels. The boiler of the same diameter went from 10ft 1in to 13ft in length. It was the first Atlantic in Britain, and unlike the LYR 4-4-2s, was outside-cylindered as in American practice.

Ivatt also designed some classes of engine around the turn of the century, which remained in service until quite late in BR steam days. The C12 Atlantic tanks and J52 0-6-0STs survived to the end of the 1950s. ∎

Ivatt C2 Atlantic tank (LNER/BR Class C12) No 1511 at Colwick shed on 23 June 1923. This engine was built with condensing apparatus for working over the Metropolitan Widened Lines, but was reallocated to Colwick in 1921.

G N R 1511

Ivatt's Atlantics

No 990 was the first locomotive of the Atlantic 4-4-2 wheel arrangement to be built in Britain, and was named *Henry Oakley* after the GNR chairman. Built in 1897, No 990, was thoroughly tested before another ten were built in 1900, followed by 10 more in 1903.

They acquired the nickname 'Klondykes'. In 1902 though, Ivatt built the first 'Large Atlantic', No 251. Its boiler was 10in larger in diameter and another 3ft 4in longer. Even the 'Large Atlantics' though, had tiny cylinders, and their tractive effort was theoretically less than that of the Stirling Singles with their generously sized cylinders.

The Atlantics were no more powerful in theoretical terms, but they had increased adhesion as a result of having twice as many driving wheels, and the bigger boiler could maintain higher steaming rates for longer.

C1 Atlantic No 4451 heads a train of Gresley-articulated Quad-Art sets at Brookmans Park in 1937. COLOUR-RAIL

Left: C1 Atlantic No 4460 at King's Cross shed in 1937. COLOUR-RAIL

Once in widespread use, the Atlantics displaced the Stirling Singles, for which little further use could be found. Some pottered about on the East Lincolnshire line for a while, but the first few years of the 20th century saw most of the Singles withdrawn and scrapped, after a relatively short life.

An Ivatt Atlantic in exchange trials with an LNWR Precursor 4-4-0 showed a 10 per cent saving in coal consumption by the Atlantic.

In 1910, Ivatt built the last batch with 18-row superheaters, not to increase power further, but to enable him to reduce boiler pressure from 175psi to 150, in order to reduce maintenance costs. Gresley added 24-element superheaters from 1912 and raised the boiler pressure to 170psi, and all eventually had 32-element superheaters to a design which originated with Robinson of the GCR.

In this form the Atlantics continued on top-link duties through the 1930s, especially on the Pullmans out of King's Cross. Other experiments tried by Gresley included, compounding and four cylinders with derived motion, but with no improvement in performance and decreased reliability. All were built at Doncaster except for the shortlived No 1300, subcontracted to Vulcan Foundry.

Only two survived to carry BR numbers, the last, No 62822 being withdrawn in November 1950. The preserved engine, No 251 was withdrawn in July 1947.

Ivatt's Atlantics were a tremendous step forward from Stirling's Singles, but that does not necessarily mean that Stirling's design was wrong in the circumstances of the 1870s. Trains simply got bigger and heavier, and the Atlantics were the ideal solution. ■

Locomotive building

Designing a steam locomotive is a complex process, handled by a large design team, using techniques perfected over many years. The railway's chief mechanical engineer takes the personal credit for all the engines built during his tenure in office, but he is really just a middleman. The Board, and the operating department make the decision as to the specification for the locomotives they require; specifying weight, size, power and speed.

The CME, in consultation with his design team, will take this specification and translate it into the physical dimensions of the engine and its vital components that affect performance, so that it complies with the stipulations for length and weight, while delivering the speed, power and economy required. The CME needs to determine the optimum boiler length, diameter and pressure, the number and diameter of wheels, and the number, diameter and stroke of the cylinders, all of which dictate the performance of the finished engine.

By comparison, building a steam locomotive is quite a simple process, albeit involving a considerable amount of heavy engineering.

First, the locomotive needs its mainframes, two identical thick steel plates with holes for the axleboxes, and to which everything else is attached. The biggest item, the boiler, is lowered onto the frames. The completed frame assembly with boiler is lowered onto the driving wheels, which are of cast iron, with steel tyres, and run in axleboxes with bronze bearings. The most complex castings are the cylinders, which are bolted to the frames. The valve gear, connecting rods and pistons, all of forged steel are fitted in place.

The boiler is of rolled steel, with usually a copper firebox, and steel boiler tubes. Once these major items are in place, the locomotive is largely complete. The cab, tender superstructure, or tanks, and the smokebox are of relatively thin steel plate, and all that is required then are front and rear carrying wheels, if applicable and the hundreds of small items which make the engine run efficiently; cab fittings, gauges, copper pipework for the lubrication system, sandboxes, chimney, whistle etc.

As a rule, all of the parts were produced 'in-house' and the locomotive assembled in the 'erecting shop'. It is said that the GER works at Stratford holds the record for assembling a new locomotive from its component parts in just over nine hours!

Different railway locomotive workshops had different techniques for locomotive building. The efficiency and reliability of a locomotive in service depended on the quality of workmanship in actually producing it. Moving parts have to be machined to very fine tolerances, and these would be specified by each individual workshop.

As locomotives got bigger and faster, one of the

crucial factors in determining the ability of a locomotive to withstand long periods of sustained high-speed running, was the lining-up of the major components, particularly the frames. It only needs a slight mis-alignment of mainframes, or twisting, with axleboxes not quite lining up, to set up huge stresses on the engine in service, leading to major failures, not just of axleboxes and valve gear components, but even including frame cracking.

Different companies perfected different techniques of optically lining up the mainframes.

In heavy engineering today, these types of technique would be handled by computers and lasers, but in the great days of steam, it was the skill of the engineers and literally a trained eye, which made the difference between an engine which would perform satisfactorily day-in, day-out for many years, and one which would not. It was widely known that two supposedly identical steam engines can perform very differently, and the reputation of a locomotive builder rested largely on the consistency of performance of its products. ■

GNR 2-6-0 No 1640 being built in the new erecting shop at Doncaster in early 1913. This corner of the works by the foreman's office was the favoured location for the construction of new types of engine. The frames carry the boiler and cylinders only at this stage, all other parts yet to be fitted.

Coach building at Doncaster

Above: GNR Howlden coach No 1283 of 1900, now preserved on the Bluebell Railway as LNER directors' saloon No 43909. BRIAN SHARPE

Below: A typical Gresley teak-panelled elliptical-roofed coach, preserved on the North Yorkshire Moors Railway. BRIAN SHARPE

Coach construction started at Doncaster as soon as the works opened in 1853. The GNR's leading role in the establishment of an Anglo-Scottish east coast route was confirmed by establishment of the East Coast Joint Stock in 1860, whereby a common pool of passenger vehicles was operated by the GNR, North Eastern and North British railways. The main express trains were the 10am departures from King's Cross and Edinburgh Waverley which began running in June 1862. By the 1870s they were known as the 'Flying Scotsman'. As

well as building for the home railway, Doncaster built coaches for the ECJS pool from 1861 to around 1900.

In 1873, Doncaster built one of the early sleeping cars and as late as 1875 its first bogie coach.

While Archibald Sturrock was both locomotive and carriage superintendent, Stirling concentrated on locomotives and Howlden was appointed carriage superintendent from 1876.

Clerestory roofs became standard from the mid-1870s and vacuum brakes from 1879. It is often forgotten that while the Stirling Singles had a reputation for speed, they were hauling express trains of four-wheeled wooden coaches with gas lighting, stoves for heating, and worst of all, no continuous brakes.

1879 saw the first dining cars manufactured in the UK produced at 'The Plant', and in 1882, Doncaster built its first corridor coach, but with no connecting gangway as yet; the corridor simply gave access to toilets at the end of the coach.

Coaches were being fitted with continuous vacuum braking by 1881. Further innovations were steam heating and buckeye couplings. Coaches began to be manufactured with steel, rather than wooden underframes from 1902.

A gentleman called Gresley, who was to prove to be

an important player in the story of 'The Plant', became carriage superintendent from 1905. His first coaches were for a small series of Railmotors being built by Ivatt. These were eventually converted to conventional coaches, though in articulated two-coach sets, and they ran until 1958.

Gresley's coaches were quickly to replace the four- and six-wheeled clerestory-roofed coaches still in widespread use on the GNR. Elliptical roofs quickly became a Gresley trademark, making GNR trains look much more modern. Electric lighting and steel underframes became standard. Articulation, where for example two coaches ran on three bogies, was not a new concept but was widely used by Gresley.

In 1911 Gresley became locomotive superintendent and Edward Thompson succeeded him in the coach department. Thompson left in 1916 for military service and did not return until 1919. His return was short-lived, and after a lot of arguing with Gresley, he left to join the NER, and was replaced by Oliver Bulleid.

After the 1923 Grouping, the post of chief mechanical engineer became the accepted norm, with the incumbent being responsible for locomotives and rolling stock.

Gresley introduced steel panelling on his coaches from 1935, and there was some variation from the varnished teak livery, particularly on the new streamlined trains. Coaches were still built largely with wooden bodywork, though on a steel underframe and with steel exterior panelling on the bodywork, but a shortage of suitable timber led to increased use of steel as opposed to wood in carriage construction.

On 21 December 1940, the carriage shop at 'The Plant' was destroyed by fire, and was not rebuilt until 1947.

Edward Thompson, who had briefly been carriage superintendent on the GNR, took over from Gresley as CME in 1941 and designed some coaches, most of which which were built after WWII in Peppercorn's reign. Naturally they were different from Gresley's, being steel-panelled, but with a conventional elliptical roof and straight ends , as opposed to having a Gresley

traditional bowed end.

After nationalisation, British Railways quickly wanted to introduce a standard design of carriage nationwide. The best features were taken from the latest designs of the 'Big Four' companies, but the new coach design looked different from any of its predecessors, though with similarities to Stanier's LMS ones and Bulleid's on the Southern. Some Doncaster features were incorporated, but overall, this was an entirely new type of carriage, and it was planned to build lots of them.

Doncaster Works was heavily involved in the production of the so-called Mk1 carriages from 1951, the first being a kitchen car, up to 1958 when the last to be built was a second-class sleeping car.

An early decision of the design team was to continue with the traditional method of construction of having a separate body from the underframe. This meant that design and construction could be shared between works, and Doncaster sometimes built coaches jointly with, for example, York. 'The Plant' built many types of coach based mostly on the BR standard Mk1 design, and this included Electric Multiple Units but never any Diesel Multiple Units, although maintenance of these was carried out and this continued for some time after all other carriage work had ceased. ∎

A BR Mk1 coach as built at Doncaster, carrying the original BR carmine and cream livery.
BRIAN SHARPE

Great Central Railway
formerly Manchester Sheffield & Lincolnshire Railway

Robinson 04 2-8-0s on freight trains were an integral part of the Doncaster railway scene right up to 1966. The National Railway Museum's 04 No 63601 can still be seen on the present-day Great Central Railway at Loughborough.
BRIAN SHARPE

The Great Northern Railway operated the north-south express route through Doncaster, but owned surprisingly little else in the area. It had its involvement in the joint line with the GER across Lincolnshire, which carried considerable coal traffic to the capital and was also used by boat trains from the north to Harwich for the Continent.

Almost simultaneously with the GNR's arrival in Doncaster, had come the South Yorkshire Railway, which was leased by the Manchester Sheffield & Lincolnshire Railway from 1861, and taken over in 1864. The MSLR, unlike some pre-Grouping railways did much as it said on the tin; it ran from Manchester to Sheffield, then on to Lincolnshire, via Retford to Lincoln, and via Doncaster to Immingham and Cleethorpes. This made it a major player in the

Doncaster area, and its acquisition jointly with the GNR of the West Riding & Grimsby Railway in 1867, gave it a share in what was the second most important route north out of the town, to Wakefield for Leeds and all the industrial wealth of the West Riding.

The SYR was conceived as a route for coal traffic from the Sheffield area to the Humber ports, and while the GNR expanded its coal traffic towards the capital, the MSLR concentrated on coal traffic to Hull and Immingham docks, passing through Doncaster in the opposite direction.

The GNR initially worked the SYR's passenger trains, and actually received approval to take over the company, but this was to ensure it continued to handle all the coal traffic originating on the route. The terms of the agreement however would have

allowed the hated Midland Railway to compete for this traffic, and Denison of the GNR persuaded the GNR not to implement the agreement for this reason.

The North Midland Railway had reached Leeds in 1840, although what we now know as the Midland Main Line from St Pancras was not completed until 1867. London (King's Cross) to Leeds via Doncaster was always potentially much quicker and there is no doubt that Leeds trains have always formed a major part of ECML services, Leeds now being a far bigger commercial centre than York, but the GNR did not have the route north of Doncaster to itself, being in joint ownership with the MSLR from Doncaster to Wakefield.

The MSLR turned itself into the Great Central Railway in 1897 as it built its main line to London (Marylebone) from Sheffield via Nottingham and Rugby. The GCR of course could now run expresses from London to York and Leeds in direct competition with the GNR and was certainly in the first division of pre-Grouping lines. Its locomotive building facility was at Gorton in Manchester, where the designs of Pollitt, and later, the very well-respected Robinson were produced, and these designs became a common sight on Doncaster's railways.

Robinson's most numerous and long-lived class, the O4 2-8-0, built for heavy coal traffic, remained in use right up to the end of steam in the Doncaster area in 1966. ■

A First Trans-Pennine Express Class 185 unit departs from Doncaster and passes Hexthorpe on what was originally the South Yorkshire Railway route into Doncaster.
BRIAN SHARPE

Right: Opposite ends of the motive power spectrum on the North Eastern Railway. Stephenson long-boilered 0-6-0 No 1275 of 1874 stands next to Bo-Bo electric No 1 (BR No 26500) in the National Railway Museum, on the site of the one-time NER York locomotive shed.
BRIAN SHARPE

North Eastern Railway

The North Eastern Railway, the middle partner in the East Coast Main Line from King's Cross to Edinburgh, had a complicated history. Formed in 1854 from the York Newcastle & Berwick, York & North Midland and Leeds Northern railways; of all the pre-Grouping companies, the NER found itself with the nearest to a total monopoly of the region it served, although it was not until 1863 that it finally absorbed its main competitor in its heartlands, the pioneering Stockton & Darlington Railway.

It seems that the NER did not initially take its role in the Anglo-Scottish main line too seriously, and it was not until 1871 that it completed its new line south from York to connect with the GNR into Doncaster, finally bringing to an end the necessity of running ECML trains over a section of the Lancashire & Yorkshire Railway. The new

NER line joined the GN at Shafthome Junction, literally a few yards south of Askern Junction where the GNR had made an end-on connection with the LYR.

This finally gave the NER its own direct access nearly into Doncaster, but even then, the NER never operated many trains to the town. The NER had originally built a line from Goole joining the MSLR at Thorne, which gave it rather indirect access to Doncaster.

The established method of operation for many ECML expresses was for the GNR engine to run through to York, and for NER engines to cover the York to Edinburgh section, including the section from Berwick. From as early as 1860, even before through services commenced between the capitals, long-distance expresses consisted of 'East Coast Joint Stock', jointly owned by the three companies. ■

Above: LNER A4 Pacific No 60009 *Union of South Africa* heads a railtour north on the former NER main line between Doncaster and Selby past Eggborough power station, near Temple Hurst Junction, on 2 December 2006. BRIAN SHARPE

Coalmining –
one of Doncaster's other industries

Doncaster's main industry after the Industrial Revolution was coal. It provided much of the impetus for building the network of railways around the town and when Doncaster made its name by building steam engines, it was the locally mined coal that provided the power. Steam engines are designed with a particular type of coal in mind, and coal from

Above: A few miles west of Doncaster, WD Austerity 2-8-0 No 90486 passes Denaby in March 1961. COLOUR-RAIL BRE 1772

Right: Freightliner Heavy Haul Class 66/5 No 66513 approaches Doncaster from the north on the ECML and crosses the River Don. The West Riding & Grimsby (GN/GC) joint line to Leeds is to the left and the Great Central avoiding line crosses the two routes just north of the river. BRIAN SHARPE

Rossington and other Doncaster collieries was known to be good for producing steam. In the great days of steam, coal was literally handpicked for particular engines for the top express jobs.

Many of the railway lines running through Doncaster never carried any meaningful passenger traffic, but much of the system remains in use today for coal traffic, despite its contraction in recent years. It was the growth of coal mining around the town that provided the incentive for a further bout of railway building in the Doncaster area in the early part of the 20th century. The GNR had little involvement in the new lines, except that it carried much of the extra coal traffic towards London.

In 1908, the Dearne Valley Railway built a line from north of Barnsley through Conisbrough and to the south of Doncaster, joining the GN and the GN/GE joint line at the complex of junctions near Black Carr. This railway remained independent but was operated first by the Hull & Barnsley Railway, then the Lancashire & Yorkshire Railway until as late as 1922 when it briefly became part of the London & North Western Railway. Always a coal-carrying line, it closed in 1966.

In 1909, the South Yorkshire Joint Railway was built, from Dinnington where it connected with a Great Central/Midland joint line from Shireoaks, near Worksop on the GCR. It ran north to cross over the meeting point of the GN, GN/GE and the Dearne Valley at Black Carr, then round the east of Doncaster to join the GCR again at Kirk Sandall. This important route for coal and other heavy freight was actually owned jointly by the GC/GN/L&Y/NE and Midland railways, thereby passing into the joint ownership of the LMS and LNER in 1923; it remains open for freight traffic today.

Another year later and a further predominantly coal-carrying line was built, by the GCR, from Hexthorpe, west of Doncaster, crossing over the GN main line just north of Doncaster station to join the GC route to Humberside. This line kept GCR freight trains away from the GNR main line through the town, and remains open today.

Another interesting line, which gave yet another pre-Grouping company more of a foothold in Doncaster, was from near Drax, crossing the GN just south of Shaftholme, then the Leeds line, with connections to the GC avoiding the line near Sprotborough before diverging again to cross the GC to Sheffield and joining yet another joint line west of Maltby. This line was a joint venture by the GCR and the Hull & Barnsley Railway, and although part was disused from the 1940's, it survived until 1969-70. This was not quite the end of railway building around

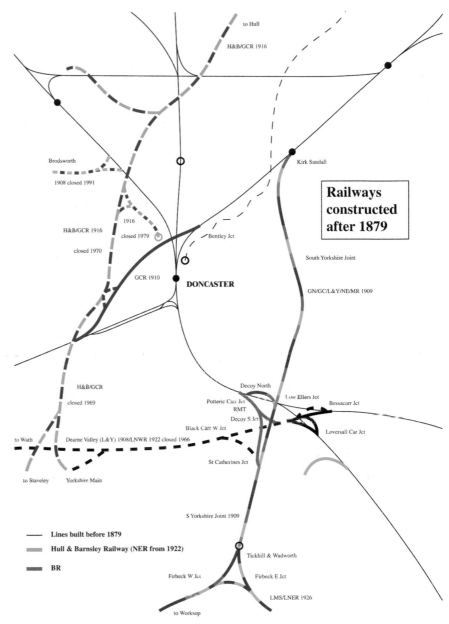

Railways constructed after 1879

— Lines built before 1879
— Hull & Barnsley Railway (NER from 1922)
— BR

Doncaster as new pits were opened and new branches built. One from the former South Yorkshire Joint Line at Tickhill to Harworth, was even promoted jointly by the LMS and LNER in 1926. ■

Below: English Electric Class 37 No 37172 heads a train of empty 16-ton mineral wagons north past Carr loco on the approach to Doncaster on 4 September 1974. BRIAN SHARPE

Gresley three-cylindered K3 2-6-0 No 61826 in ex-works condition after overhaul at Doncaster in April 1958. COLOUR-RAIL BRE 1484

Herbert Nigel Gresley –
Locomotive superintendent of the GNR

Sir Nigel Gresley

Gresley is the man who must be credited with really putting Doncaster on the map. His engines may not have actually outshone his competitors' any more than those of his predecessors did on the Great Northern, but his flair together with that of the GNR's successor, the LNER and its publicity machine, made them appear top of the league, a reputation that is still considered by many to be true to this day.

In the late 19th century, there were numerous pre-Grouping railway companies, each with its own principal locomotive works. Already, the GNR's Doncaster works was in the first division, Patrick Stirling's and later, Henry Ivatt's locomotive designs

had seen to that. But there were other works turning out comparable engines. By the time of the Grouping in 1923, it probably has to be accepted, that Swindon was the clear leader.

Herbert Nigel Gresley was born on 19 June 1876 at 14 Dublin Street, Edinburgh, one of three children of the Rev Nigel Gresley and his wife, Joanna. After leaving Marlborough College, Gresley was employed as an apprentice by the London & North Western Railway at Crewe, on his 17th birthday, working under the much-feared Francis Webb.

In 1898, he moved on to the Lancashire & Yorkshire Railway, and eventually rose to the position of carriage and wagon superintendent. Gresley

Gresley should succeed him as the GNR's locomotive engineer, and the board agreed. The railway industry waited to see whether he would be as forward-thinking and innovative with his locomotive designs as he had been with his carriages. Ivatt was a well-respected engineer, and his engines were good, but at the time they were not the best in Britain.

Gresley's first steam locomotive design for the GNR was the H1 (later LNER K1) 2-6-0 in 1912. They were conventional engines, in traditional GNR style, and designed to accelerate long-distance goods traffic. As early as 1915, though, Gresley was thinking about a four-cylindered Pacific for express trains; unfortunately, wartime was not a good time to build such a thing.

In 1918, Gresley designed the O1 2-8-0 for heavy-freight traffic, and these not only had three cylinders but also Gresley's new design of conjugated valve gear.

This was to set the scene for Gresley's locomotives in the future, but he had yet to build an express engine. Partly this was because Ivatt's Atlantics were good and held in such high regard by Gresley that he felt he had little need to improve on them immediately, but it was also because the GNR was in need of more modern freight power.

When Gresley's first express engine did appear, in 1920, the H4 was a 2-6-0 – not a wheel arrangement normally associated with express power, particularly on level tracks. It was built for sustained power output, not high speed, with three cylinders and six small driving wheels, which gave room for a huge boiler. The class was to be reclassified K3 by the LNER. When they were built, they were huge express engines that shocked everyone in the railway industry by their sheer size.

This was very much a forestaste of what was to come. The GNR's track had, by now, improved but the civil engineer still had grave reservations about the effect Gresley's monstrous engines might have on his track and bridges. ∎

Below: Gresley two-cylindered K2 2-6-0 NP 37o 4691 *Loch Morar* at Mallaig in 1936. COLOUR-RAIL

married Ethel Frances Fullagar in 1901.

After an interview with its locomotive engineer, HA Ivatt, and on the recommendation of John Aspinall of the LYR, Gresley joined the GNR as assistant carriage and wagon superintendent in January 1905.

He quickly made his mark on the GNR. His design of elliptical-roofed, steel-framed and teak-bodied coaches was introduced within a year and became standard for the GNR and for the East Coast Joint Stock on the Scottish expresses. The last ones were still in use on British Railways' express trains into the mid-1970s.

In 1911, at the age of 35, Ivatt recommended that

1923 *The Grouping*
London & North Eastern Railway

Ivatt D2 4-4-0 No 4337 and C1 Atlantic No 3272 at Hitchin in 1937.
COLOUR-RAIL NE16

There had been ongoing mergers and takeovers in the railway industry, with plans for major mergers that would have created much larger companies. WWI accelerated the process and government intervention dictated that there would be simultaneous planned mergers for the sake of financial stability, because a healthy railway system was essential to the nation's economy.

All of the independent pre-Grouping railway companies were merged in 1923 into just four – the Great Western Railway, the Southern Railway, the London Midland & Scottish Railway and the London & North Eastern Railway.

Doncaster was firmly in LNER territory as it was the meeting point of the GNR, GCR, GER and NER all of which became the principal English constituents of the new company. The only lines where there was an LMS involvement in the area was in the case of the LYR. It had become part of the LNWR a year earlier and ran to Askern Junction to the north, and via the old Dearne Valley line, to the complex of junctions at Bessacarr to the south. There was also the South Yorkshire Joint Line, skirting the town to the east which became the joint responsibility of the LMS and LNER.

Operationally, it was clearly much more sensible for the London to Edinburgh expresses to be operated by one company throughout, but apart from that, there was initially little change and ex-GCR lines and ex-GNR lines remained quite autonomous.

The biggest impact on Doncaster and 'The Plant' though was that a new post of chief mechanical engineer was created for the new company, and the job went to Gresley, already top man at Doncaster, but now in a position of much greater authority within a much bigger organisation.

'The Plant' of course quickly rose in stature as a

result of Gresley's appointment although he moved his office from Doncaster to King's Cross on formation of the LNER, and travelled to work daily by train. He made a point of being in regular contact with the drivers.

Despite not being based there, Gresley inevitably considered 'The Plant' to be the premier locomotive workshops on the LNER, responsible now for producing locomotives for a railway which ran from King's Cross right up to Fraserburgh, Lossiemouth and Mallaig, not just York, Leeds and Bradford. Gresley's A1 Pacific design, which appeared just before the Grouping, was no doubt intended by Gresley as the future standard for express haulage throughout much of the LNER system.

Locomotive and carriage liveries changed, but not by too much. Both the GNR and NER had apple green-liveried engines, although the GNR ones had dark green edging to the tenders, and brown frames. A simplified version of apple green, lined in black and white was adopted, for passenger engines at least. Renumbering took place with GNR engines mostly having 3000 added to their numbers.

GNR coaches were finished in varnished teak, but NER ones were liveried in maroon. The GCR used varnished teak, and the GER had recently changed from maroon to teak. Teak was adopted as standard by the LNER, with little effect on the appearance of ECML expresses as the East Coast Joint Stock already in use was in teak livery throughout.

Once in charge of locomotive design on the LNER in 1923, Gresley could really make his mark. He became acquainted with other locomotive engineers

in this country and abroad, and paid attention to their advice. Although he had designed his own conjugated valve gear for three-cylindered engines, he added details recommended by Holcroft of the South Eastern & Chatham Railway, to really perfect the design. Three-cylinder propulsion, with conjugated valve gear became a Gresley trademark and will always be associated with Doncaster.

Gresley's assistant was Oliver Bulleid, who was to become one of the most innovative locomotive engineers ever to have practised his trade in Britain. He had joined the GNR in 1901 as a premium apprentice, and was later to achieve fame in his own right on the Southern Railway. Bulleid was married to HA Ivatt's eldest daughter. ■

Gresley's Pacifics

Gresley first designed a couple of good, but not outstanding locomotives for the GNR, but people had taken notice of his new express engine, the H4, later LNER K3. It was only a 2-6-0 but it was huge, and it had three cylinders, already a Gresley trademark.

The man did not then progress to 2-6-2s or 4-6-0s but went straight to a 4-6-2, known as a Pacific. It was not the first Pacific to run in Britain; the GWR had led the way but found its engine to be of limited usefulness. The NER also built five Pacifics at the same time as Gresley's two GNR ones, but just as these all took to the rails came the Grouping, and decision time as to who would be the chief mechanical engineer (CME) of the new London & North Eastern Railway Company.

Gresley was favourite, but he favoured Robinson from the GCR. Certainly Raven on the NER was considered too old, and in the end Gresley's youth saw him appointed in preference to Robinson.

Gresley's A1 Pacifics were then thoroughly tested against Raven's, now classified A2, while Doncaster continued to build A1s anyway. Perhaps inevitably, it was the Doncaster Pacifics that were clearly superior and the LNER then started turning them out in considerable numbers.

Stylistically, the similarity with the H4 (K3) was evident, but Gresley had to compromise with his Pacific design; it was not quite as he wanted it; everywhere weight could be saved, it was, even to the extent of using a lower boiler pressure than would have been ideal. The new engine when it emerged from Doncaster works in 1922, carrying the number 1470, was considered so important that the GNR even gave it a name – *Great Northern*. Partly this was to keep the company name alive as the GNR was soon to disappear into the London & North Eastern Railway. But what had been an imaginative choice of name for the company was really rather less-than-inspiring for the locomotive.

A second engine followed, No 1471, and this was to be given the even-less-interesting name of *Sir Frederick Banbury*, after the chairman of the GNR who had been so opposed to the Grouping. There was no real plan for naming the engines and the LNER generally turned them out unnamed.

However, a decision was made to name a third engine for display at the Wembley Exhibition of 1924. No 1472 was named after the LNER's premier express train, the 'Flying Scotsman'. This was a title that had been given unofficially to the GNR's 10am

departure from King's Cross to Edinburgh, but was not adopted officially until 1927.

It also happens to sound like a good name for a racehorse, and the town of Doncaster was famous for two things – horseracing and building steam engines.

When *Flying Scotsman* appeared at the British Empire Exhibition at Wembley in 1924, it stood next to the GWR's 4-6-0 No 4073 *Caerphilly Castle*, which the GWR's publicity described as Britain's most powerful express engine. Gresley was not actually consulted to any real extent, but the LNER directors arranged for the A1 Pacific to be scientifically tested against Collett's GWR Castles on both LNER and GWR routes to try to prove which really was the most powerful. Certainly the Castle was considered to be the pinnacle of locomotive design in Britain, although they were only 4-6-0s. The Castle won in this contest, particularly in terms of economy, so there was obviously still room for improvement in the LNER design.

The two designs had been produced for very different routes and to use very different types of coal, so they were difficult to compare. Churchward of the Great Western was considered top in the

LNER A3 Pacific No 60091 *Captain Cuttle* on an up non-stop express, speeds through Doncaster station in 1952. COLOUR-RAIL BRE680

league of locomotive engineers at the time, and his engineering traditions were continued by Collett. Gresley took the lessons of the locomotive exchanges on board, in particular the use of long-lap piston valves. This, together with increasing the boiler pressure from 180 to 220psi, increasing the amount of superheating, and slightly reducing cylinder diameter, transformed the A1s. In doing so, Gresley transformed his own design from a good engine into arguably the best in Britain.

Swindon was the leader in steam locomotive design in 1923. Crewe and Derby were building little of note and none of the Southern Railway's designs were very exciting, but the SR came up with the Lord Nelsons in 1926 which the LMS virtually copied as its Royal Scot. These were both massive, powerful and reliable engines, but without the speed or style of either Swindon or Doncaster products, and they were still only 4-6-0s.

Gresley took over towards the end of the Great Northern Railway's independent existence and made his mark just before the GNR became part of the LNER, after which circumstances changed considerably. The LNER kept most of its inherited locomotive workshops open, some continuing

locomotive building, particularly the ex-NER facility at Darlington. Gresley, having become CME was in overall charge of locomotive design and building at both, but as Gresley was ex-GNR, it was inevitable that Darlington would always play second fiddle to Doncaster.

Doncaster's real competition therefore was now from the main works of the other three of the Big Four companies. The GWR concentrated its locomotive building at Swindon. The LMS continued with Crewe and Derby, with assistance mainly from Horwich, while the SR continued to build engines at all of the three it inherited, Ashford, Brighton and Eastleigh.

GWR locomotive design did not actually progress much after 1923, although it was already so good at that stage that not only did it heavily influence the LMS when Stanier moved from Swindon to Crewe, but Gresley learned a lot of useful lessons about the finer points of locomotive design. Under different circumstances, Swindon could and should have stayed in the lead, but once Gresley had taken some of the best ideas on board, it was Doncaster that set the pace for progress in the heyday of steam, kept on its toes by competition mainly from Crewe. ■

Flying Scotsman
Is it an engine or a train?

Doncaster will always be synonymous with the 'Flying Scotsman', the train and more particularly the engine. When the 'Flying Scotsman' train first ran in 1864, Doncaster was not even a stop en route; the train was scheduled non-stop Retford to York, though later Doncaster was served by a slip coach detached on the move.

It was not until 1867 that the engines that pulled the 'Flying Scotsman', at least between King's Cross and York, began to be built at Doncaster. At that time, the train was officially the 10am from King's Cross and was unofficially called the 'Flying Scotsman' only by the public.

In 1923, when the newly formed LNER put its latest express steam engine, No 1472 on display at an exhibition at Wembley, the LNER broke with the tradition it had inherited from the GNR, and gave the engine a name – *Flying Scotsman*.

In 1927, the LNER finally gave in to public demand and named the 10am departure from King's Cross officially; the name 'Flying Scotsman' started to appear in timetables and a headboard was carried on the front of the locomotive.

And so started years of confusion in the public's mind over whether *Flying Scotsman* is an engine or a train. In fact in 1927, the engine No 4472 *Flying Scotsman* would frequently carry the headboard as it hauled the 'Flying Scotsman' train.

It did not haul the very first working of the express to officially carry the name, the relief working of which achieved considerable fame for the LNER by running non-stop to Newcastle.

Flying Scotsman itself was chosen though for the inaugural non-stop King's Cross to Edinburgh 'Flying Scotsman' on 1 May 1928. This was not actually a record non-stop run by a steam engine, but was the longest to be scheduled for regular daily operation.

The name 'Flying Scotsman' caught the public's imagination to such an extent that *Flying Scotsman* the engine, was always selected by the LNER wherever possible for any of its publicity stunts, despite it not actually being regarded as one of the best-performing engines in the class. In 1934 though, it was *Flying Scotsman*, not any other A1 Pacific which became the first fully authenticated world record-breaker of the 100mph barrier.

The A1 class was developed into the A3, which had long-travel valves and a higher boiler pressure. Later engines were built to A3 specifications, and the earlier ones were eventually converted. A few were temporarily reclassified A10 before their conversion.

Gresley intended to introduce a new, long-distance, high-speed train service in 1935 and conducted some tests with A1 and A3 Pacifics, during which first *Flying Scotsman* reached 100mph, then *Papyrus* 108mph.

On 30 November 1934, with renowned driver William Sparshatt in charge, A1 No 4472 took four coaches 185.8 miles from King's Cross to Leeds in 151 mins and six seconds. Another two coaches were added and, between Little Bytham in Lincolnshire and Essendine in Rutland, No 4472 is claimed to have broken the 100mph barrier.

In March 1935, again with driver Sparshatt at the regulator, A3 No 2750 with six coaches ran from King's Cross to Newcastle and back. The 500 miles were covered in 423 mins and 23 seconds, including 300 miles at 80mph average. In fact, *Papyrus'* feat is considered genuine by historians while *Flying*

Scotsman's maximum speed is a little questionable, but it is *Flying Scotsman* which became famous, while *Papyrus* was always just another Gresley Pacific.

Flying Scotsman the engine, was based for almost all of its 40-year working life in London, and the 'Flying Scotsman' train never normally stopped at Doncaster (or anywhere else), but 'The Plant' at Doncaster had built a steam engine which was already arguably the most famous steam engine in the world, a title it would retain and build on over the years, despite bigger, faster and more powerful ones being built, both at Doncaster and elsewhere. ∎

No 4472 *Flying Scotsman* at 'The Plant' on 29 November 1924 after the first Wembley exhibition.

A3 Pacific No 60041 *Salmon Trout*, newly converted to double chimney but not yet fitted with smoke deflectors, stands in the bay platform at Doncaster.
DAVID HOPPER

The racehorses –
real ones and locomotives

Horses played a vital role in Doncaster's history, being a major centre on the Great North Road for the stagecoach trade. Horseracing in the town dates from 1703, and the famed four-day St Leger meeting from 1776.

The St Leger was to provide a tremendous impetus for the early railway builders, nearly every route into the town opening just in time for that year's St Leger in September. With no road competition, the railway traffic at its peak for St Leger week was phenomenal. Coal traffic was suspended, the yards cleared

and up to 70,000 people descended on Doncaster by train daily, the yards being filled with trains from all directions and many different companies, awaiting their return journeys.

Naming of locomotives was not an accepted practice on the Great Northern Railway, nor on most of the railways whose engines worked into Doncaster, with the exception of the Great Central. However, the GNR had named the pioneer Ivatt Atlantic No 990 *Henry Oakley*, and in 1922 in view of the imminent Grouping also named its first Pacific, No 1470 *Great Northern*. The

LNER named the second, No 1471 *Sir Frederick Banbury*, after the last GNR chairman (and an outspoken opponent of Grouping).

The first chairman of the LNER was William Whitelaw and he brought with him from the North British Railway, a tradition of naming both trains and engines. The first Pacific completed by the LNER, No 1472, remained unnamed initially but when chosen for display at the 1924 British Empire Exhibition at Wembley, it was given the name *Flying Scotsman*, then the unofficial name of the 10am King's Cross to Edinburgh express.

A decision was eventually taken to continue naming the A1 Pacifics, and the theme chosen was racehorses; very appropriate in view of their speed potential and Doncaster's long association with horseracing.

The majority was allocated the names of winners of the St Leger at Doncaster, but it was actually a very inconsistent policy, and some simply sounded like racehorses but were not (like *Flying Scotsman*, and later *Dick Turpin*). One or two of the Pacifics carried names of people such as *William Whitelaw* and *Prince of Wales*. Most though carried the charismatic names that became such an integral part of the East Coast Main Line scene for the next 40 years.

In fact, it is still fascinating to read the roll of honour on the wall of the bar at Doncaster racecourse, where the list of winners reads almost like the Ian Allan Locospotter's Book, continuing from the Gresley Pacifics right through to the Deltic diesels and beyond. ■

The Gresley A1, later A3 class in order of construction, with later BR numbers

Class			Number & Name		Class		Number & Name
A1	1470	4470	60113 Great Northern		A1/A10/A3	2572	60073 St Gatien
A1/A3	1471	4471	60102 Sir Frederick Banbury		A1/A3	2573	60074 Harvester
A1/A10/A3	1471	4472	60103 Flying Scotsman		A1/A3	2574	60075 St Frusquin
A1/A3	1473	4473	60104 Solario		A1/A3	2575	60076 Galopin
A1/A3	1474	4474	60105 Victor Wild		A1/A3	2576	60077 The White Night
A1/A10/A3	1475	4475	60106 Flying Fox		A1/A3	2577	60078 Night Hawk
A1/A10/A3	1476	4476	60107 Royal Lancer		A1/A3	2578	60079 Bayardo
A1/A3	1477	4477	60108 Gay Crusader		A1/A3	2579	60080 Dick Turpin
A1/A3	1478	4478	60109 Hermit		A1/A3	2580	60081 Shotover
A1/A3	1479	4479	60110 Robert the Devil		A1/A3	2581	60082 Neil Gow
A1/A3	1480	4480	60111 Enterprise		A1/A3	2582	60083 Sir Hugo
A1/A10/A3	1481	4481	60112 St Simon		A3	2743	60089 Felstead
A1/A10/A3		2543	60044 Melton		A3	2744	60090 Grand Parade
A1/A3		2544	60045 Lemberg		A3	2745	60091 Captain Cuttle
A1/A3		2545	60046 Diamond Jubilee		A3	2746	60092 Fairway
A1/A10/A3		2546	60047 Donovan		A3	2747	60093 Coronach
A1/A10/A3		2547	60048 Doncaster		A3	2748	60094 Colorado
A1/A10/A3		2548	60049 Galtee More		A3	2749	60095 Flamingo
A1/A3		2549	60050 Persimmon		A3	2750	60096 Papyrus
A1/A3		2550	60051 Blink Bonny		A3	2751	60097 Humorist
A1/A3		2551	60052 Prince Palatine		A3	2752	60098 Spion Kop
A1/A3		2552	60053 Sansovino		A3	2595	60084 Trigo
A1/A10/A3		2553	60054 Manna / Prince of Wales		A3	2596	60085 Manna
A1/A3		2554	60055 Woolwinder		A3	2597	60086 Gainsborough
A1/A3		2555	60056 Centenary		A3	2598	60087 Blenheim
A1/A10/A3		2556	60057 Ormonde		A3	2599	60088 Book Law
A1/A10/A3		2557	60058 Blair Athol		A3	2795	60099 Call Boy
A1/A3		2558	60059 Tracery		A3	2796	60100 Spearmint
A1/A3		2559	60060 The Tetrarch		A3	2797	60101 Cicero
A1/A3		2560	60061 Pretty Polly		A3	2500	60035 Windsor Lad
A1/A3		2561	60062 Minoru		A3	2501	60036 Colombo
A1/A10/A3		2562	60063 Isinglass		A3	2502	60037 Hyperion
A1/A3		2563	60064 William Whitelaw/Tagalie		A3	2503	60038 Firdaussi
A1/A10/A3		2564	60065 Knight of Thistle		A3	2504	60039 Sandwich
A1/A10/A3		2565	60066 Merry Hampton		A3	2505	60040 Brown Jack
A1/A3		2566	60067 Ladas		A3	2506	60041 Salmon Trout
A1/A10/A3		2567	60068 Sir Visto		A3	2507	60042 Singapore
A1/A3		2568	60069 Sceptre		A3	2508	60043 Brown Jack
A1/A10/A3		2569	60070 Gladiateur				
A1/A3		2570	60071 Tranquil				
A1/A3		2571	60072 Sunstar				

All of the A1/A3 class were built at 'The Plant' at Doncaster, apart from Nos 2563 to 2582 that were subcontracted to North British in Glasgow.

Steam preservation
A museum opens at York

Just two years after the formation of the LNER in 1923 came the centenary of the opening of the Stockton & Darlington Railway. This railway was the first public railway in the world to be operated by steam traction, and although it actually first ran from Shildon not Darlington, through to Stockton, it continued to grow and its empire briefly stretched right across the Pennines to Tebay and Penrith. Until it was eventually swallowed up in the empire of the North Eastern Railway which surrounded it on all sides.

The NER had staged an exhibition and cavalcade of locomotives in 1875 on the 50th anniversary of the opening of the Stockton & Darlington Railway, in which the original *Locomotion No 1,* already effectively preserved by the NER, appeared in steam. In 1925 of course, the S&D of 1825 was part of the LNER, and if the centenary was to be commemorated, it would be by the LNER.

At that time of course, the concept of railway preservation as we now know it was unheard of, but a surprising number of historic steam engines had been kept for posterity by a variety of custodians, including

of course *Locomotion No 1.* The LNER arranged another exhibition of historic and new steam engines and stock from railways all over the country, and staged a memorable cavalcade of engines and stock between Shildon and Darlington.

The 'Big Four' were noted as having differing attitudes to the preservation of historic locomotives when withdrawn, the GWR and later the LMS behaving in particularly cavalier fashions. The LNER had inherited a number of engines of S&D or NER origin, preserved largely as a result of their participation in the NER's 1875 event. Gresley on the LNER was known to have a benevolent attitude to his predecessors' designs and even before Gresley took over as locomotive superintendent, Ivatt had ensured that Stirling's pioneer 8ft Single No 1 was put aside for posterity at Doncaster.

The lasting legacy of the LNER's staging of the 1925 S&D centenary event was the establishment of a permanent museum for the display of the now-significant number of engines in its possession, mostly of S&D or NER origin. The location selected was

The replica of *Locomotion No 1,* which had hauled the opening train on the world's first steam-worked public railway in 1825, led the Shildon cavalcade in 1875.
BRIAN SHARPE

Doncaster's Railway Legends

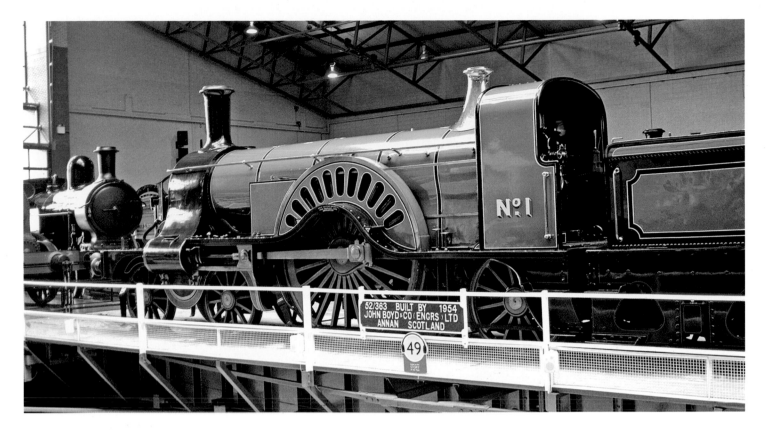

GNR No 1 stands on the turntable in the National Railway Museum at York.
BRIAN SHARPE

York, not too far from Doncaster, and it has to be said, more of a tourist venue. Nevertheless, one of Doncaster's most-celebrated products, GNR No 1 went into the museum in 1926 and entered the world of permanent public preservation.

Added to the display in the next few years were the London Brighton & South Coast Railway's 0-4-2 No 214 *Gladstone*, and the Great Western's record-breaking 4-4-0 No 3440 *City of Truro*. The LNER was a little biased in its choice of further exhibits, Ivatt's pioneer Atlantic No 990 *Henry Oakley*, and the larger No 251 from Doncaster being found places, along with a classic NER 4-4-0 No 1621, but nothing from the GCR, GER or NBR, although a NBR Atlantic was considered.

By 1948 though, three of Doncaster's best-known products from its GNR years were in preservation, and unlike some 'preserved' engines elsewhere, had survived WWII. British Railways was soon to establish a much more methodical approach to the preservation of historic relics, but Doncaster's famous big express engines were still at the height of their careers, any thought of preservation being in the far-distant future.

Nevertheless the seeds were well and truly sown, and when steam was finally displaced by more modern motive power, a selection of Doncaster's most celebrated products escaped the scrapman, and continued to do the job they were built for – pulling heavy trains – and fast. ∎

GNR Stirling Single No 1, though not in steam, is hauled by another Doncaster-built celebrity; A4 Pacific No 4498 *Sir Nigel Gresley* at the cavalcade staged as the climax to the Stockton & Darlington 150th anniversary celebrations on 31 August 1975. BRIAN SHARPE

LNER P1 2-8-2 No 2393 at
New Barnet in 1937.
COLOUR-RAIL NE25

Goods engines

Gresley O2 2-8-0 No 63974
ex-works after overhaul at
Doncaster. GAVIN MORRISON

Its express engines capture the public's imagination, but express trains were not the lifeblood of most railways. Railways were built for the transport of heavy freight, especially coal, and passenger traffic came second, although it was the railways which first made long-distance high-speed travel possible and created the demand for it. Nevertheless, it was the continuing movement of heavy freight that made the profits for the railway companies.

While the famous locomotive workshops such as Doncaster, Crewe and Swindon produced the glamorous named express engines, far more of their resources were actually allocated to building and maintaining huge fleets of engines that simply hauled coal, day-in, day-out for their whole lives, and were of no less importance to their owners. They needed to be as efficient and reliable as possible to keep the vast tonnages on the move.

Gresley continued his big engine policy in the early days of the LNER and followed his Pacifics with a three-cylinder 2-8-2 version for freight service. But the two P1s were simply too powerful for their own good and could haul coal trains that were so long they brought all other trains to a standstill until they were out of the way. Gresley was a little ahead of his time, and had to moderate his ambitions in terms of goods engines. ■

Not built at Doncaster

GNR J52 0-6-0ST No 1247 of 1899 vintage was the first main line steam locomotive to be purchased from BR for preservation by a private individual, the late Capt Bill Smith RN, but it was not a Doncaster-built example. The Sharp Stewart, Glasgow-built engine is now in the National Collection, and on display at Locomotion: the National Railway Museum at Shildon. BRIAN SHARPE

Darlington-designed, North British-built, but Doncaster-maintained, the LNER Gresley B17 4-6-0s were Gresley's attempt to accelerate Great Eastern line expresses out of Liverpool Street. No 61636 *Harlaxton Manor* stands ex-works at Doncaster in 1950. COLOUR-RAIL BRE 1591

M ost of the pre-Grouping railways, and the Big Four, subcontracted some of their locomotive building to outside contractors. The GNR and LNER pursued this course of action as much as any other railways if not more, and it is surprising how many well-known classes and locomotives were not actually built at Doncaster.

Although the preserved GNR tender engines, 4-2-2 No 1 and Atlantics No 990 and No 251 were Doncaster-built, the two surviving GNR tank engines were not. J52 0-6-0ST No 1247 was built by Sharp Stewart in 1899, and N2 0-6-2T

The solitary LNER Beyer-Garratt 2-8-2+2-8-2 No 69999 awaits scrapping at Doncaster works in March 1956. This engine was originally conceived as an articulated pair of Great Central Railway O4 2-8-0s. After the Grouping, Gresley specified an articulated version of two GNR O2s, but it was built by Beyer Peacock, holder of the patent for the articulated design, and never performed as well as engines to the company's own design did abroad.
GAVIN MORRISON

No 69523 was built by North British in 1921, both were built in Glasgow.

In LNER days, Doncaster considered itself the senior locomotive works for new construction, although Darlington built rather more and very occasionally other works participated, such as when Gorton built some B1 4-6-0s. Of Gresley-designed classes for example, the K4 2-6-0s and D49 4-4-0s were built at Darlington, while the B17 4-6-0s, designed at Darlington were built by North British.

Even 20 of the original Gresley A1 Pacifics were subcontracted to North British, and construction of the Peppercorn A1 Pacifics was shared between Doncaster and Darlington. All the Peppercorn A2s were built at Doncaster, as were the original P2 2-8-2s later rebuilt to Pacifics, but the A2/1s were Darlington-built.

Thompson's B1 4-6-0s and Peppercorn's K1 2-6-0s were largely North British-built, including the preserved examples; B1s Nos 61264 and 1306, and K1 No 62005. ∎

Experimental locomotives

By the time of the Grouping, all the pre-1923 companies had well-designed, fast, efficient steam engines, some slightly more so than others. Locomotive design development in the early years of the Big Four seemed to centre largely on how big an engine could be produced while basically following existing designs.

When Gresley was on the GNR he was probably at the forefront of innovative design, in that his two Pacifics were not only the biggest in regular express service at the time but they incorporated other fairly drastic departures from established design criteria.

However, after moving to the LNER he did not stand still during his time there; at first his Pacifics were not as good as they could have been, and drawing on a variety of sources, including Swindon and the US, he set out to improve them, to the point where they were developed into among the best, if not the best, express steam locomotives ever built in Britain.

They were still basically a conventional steam engine, and Gresley among others, experimented with various deviations from accepted steam locomotive design practice.

Perhaps the most drastic was the W1 Class 4-6-4 No 10000, an engine that also introduced the concept of streamlining. This unorthodox experiment saw the use of a marine-type water tube boiler at a pressure of no less than 450psi. Built at Darlington rather than Doncaster, the 'Hush-Hush' as it became known, as details were somewhat secretive, No 10000 did only a limited amount of test running, before storage and eventual rebuilding to a conventional, though unique, streamlined 4-6-4.

It was not a success but it was something that a railway somewhere needed to experiment with as it could have totally revolutionised steam locomotive design. At least Gresley was not afraid to try it, while his contemporaries were playing safe with designs that were good, strong, powerful, reliable and economical, but somehow lacked the vision and star quality that only Gresley seemed able to produce.

Gresley's conjugated valve gear for three-cylinder propulsion was already fairly radical, but he continued to develop even more unusual ideas, for example experimenting with rotary-cam poppet valve gear on his P2 2-8-2 design.

Gresley visited America and Germany, and also became friendly with Chapelon, the noted French engineer. He used ideas from these sources to further enhance his designs. Many of the more radical ideas were incorporated into this second three-cylinder 2-8-2 design, the first of which carried the name *Cock o' the North*, designed to haul heavy trains on the Edinburgh-Aberdeen route.

With Lenz poppet valve gear, a feed-water heater, Kylchap double blastpipe and chimney and a semi-streamlined appearance, this was a distinctive engine. It and its classmates, which did not all incorporate the experimental innovations, were again just too big for the line they ran on, but they kept Gresley's name in the headlines.

Meanwhile William Stanier had moved from Swindon to Crewe and the LMS star began to rise

and give the LNER some serious competition, but it could be said that Stanier's engines were just enlarged Great Western ones, with little real innovation at first.

However, while Gresley tried to move steam locomotive technology forward at Doncaster, Stanier later did as much, if not more, at Crewe, building for example the 'Turbomotive' No 6202, with steam turbine drive.

The next stage of course was to move on from steam completely, and all of the Big Four started to look into diesel engines as the means of traction for the future. Gresley looked at Germany's 'Flying Hamburger' diesel units, but decided there was nothing to be gained, and pressed on with his A4 streamliner instead. The Second World War delayed the innovations, which were clearly just around the corner, and neither Doncaster's, nor Crewe's radical steam ideas were ever really given a chance. ■

Gresley's 'Hush-Hush' W1 No 10000 was rebuilt as a conventional engine, but was not an A4 and it remained un-named. Allocated to Doncaster in the 1950s, it had a regular diagram, working from the town to King's Cross and back for several years. No 60700 stands in the now-roofless Carr loco in 1958.
COLOUR-RAIL BRE145

Carr loco

LNER A4 4-6-2 No 60017 *Silver Fox* at Doncaster shed on 29 April 1962.
GAVIN MORRISON
LNER A1 4-6-2 No 60122 *Curlew* at Doncaster shed on 29 April 1962.
GAVIN MORRISON

Doncaster had an atmosphere all of its own, the names were familiar to enthusiasts of many generations; 'The Plant', the Crimpsall shops, Decoy yard, and Carr loco.

One of the biggest on the GNR, the LNER and BR's Eastern Region, Doncaster locomotive sheds at The Carr were an important part of the town's contribution to keeping the trains moving.

Comparatively few long-distance expresses ever started from Doncaster, and the town was never one of the major locomotive-changing points on the ECML. Throughout most of the steam era, expresses changed engines at Grantham, York and Newcastle, giving approximately 100 miles of running each, which was considered the optimum before servicing was required, and prevented engines from straying too far from their home bases.

Doncaster was not therefore the home of many of the Pacifics it had built; the shed catered primarily for the vast numbers of freight engines serving the collieries in the area.

Although four A4s were allocated new to Doncaster, this was shortlived and the Carr never had a large Pacific allocation. In 1950, it was just six A3s, but this grew as new A1s were built and in 1959, there were seven A3s and 13 A1s, plus the W1 4-6-4 No 60700. ∎

O2 2-8-0 No 63943 on shed in untypically clean condition in June 1962. COLOUR-RAIL BRE1889

Below: LNER A2 4-6-2 No 60533 *Happy Knight* at Doncaster shed. COLOUR-RAIL BRE529

The world-beating LNER A4 4-6-2 No 60022 *Mallard* on the turntable at Doncaster shortly before withdrawal from service on 17 June 1962. GAVIN MORRISON

Doncaster station

LMS 8F 2-8-0 No 48151 heads non-stop through Doncaster with a railtour for York on 3 February 2007. A batch of these Stanier LMS engines was built at Doncaster during the war. BRIAN SHARPE

The layout of the present Doncaster station is remarkably little changed from the GNR station of 1850. Four tracks through the middle, two main platforms, and a central crossover, still remain and have simply been expanded on.

The triangular junction with the South Yorkshire Railway, south of the station, dates back to 1849, but the major change to the main line layout since 1850 was to the north. First the MSLR came in from the north-east, then the West Riding & Grimsby from the north-west, but even with three major routes from cities to the north, it was all funnelled into just two tracks, which were crossed on the level by the Great North Road immediately north of the station. It must have been the level crossing from hell! And of course at this time, there was no avoiding line,

and all coal trains ran through the station.

A bridge was eventually built to carry the main road over the railway in 1909-11, and new railway bridges over the Don were built to enable extra tracks eventually to be laid for Leeds trains.

The footbridge was replaced by a subway in 1939, when a new platform 1 was built making an island platform. The Hull line was separated by turning sidings into main lines in around 1940, but the war intervened and put a stop to further developments.

Incredibly, it was 1949 before the new track was laid over the river on the bridge installed 40 years earlier, to finally give Leeds trains separate tracks.

BR invested £125,000 in modernizing the station in the early 1970s, building a new travel centre in the concourse and a £4m investment in 2007 has further enhanced the station's facilities. ∎

An example of Gresley's first three cylindered design, LNER K3 2-6-0 No 61828 leaves for Lincoln on 27 June 1959. GAVIN MORRISON

Class 31 No 31187 heads a short empty stock train south through Doncaster on 21 April 1976. BRIAN SHARPE

Doncaster station today.

The A4s –
The streamlined Pacifics

By 1937, Gresley's A3 Pacifics, the refined version of the A1s, were masters of the ECML and elsewhere, but Gresley felt he could do even better without deviating from the successful formula. The LNER intended introducing a new high-speed service; Gresley produced the A4 Pacific, essentially an A3 with some further enhancements to the vital dimensions, to give a little extra power and speed. What made the A4s different though, was their appearance – they were streamlined.

It is said that Gresley was a traditionalist and not particularly interested in streamlining his engines, and this feature of the A4 design was mainly attributable to Sir Ralph Wedgwood, then LNER chairman, with input from Gresley's flamboyant assistant Oliver Bulleid. Unlike other classes of Pacific, the A4s were exclusively built at Doncaster.

The basic design of the A4 was similar to the A3 but with a higher boiler pressure, at 250psi, and slightly reduced cylinder diameter, to give greater power. The streamlined casing, inspired by the shape of a Bugatti racing car and perfected in wind-tunnel tests, set off with a silver colour scheme, made the first A4 the most striking steam engine ever seen, in Britain at least. It is actually questionable whether streamlining made the engines any faster, but it certainly aroused huge media interest.

The engines were designed to work the new 'Silver Jubilee' the 232.3 miles from Darlington to King's Cross at an average of 70.4mph, only slightly slower than the GWR's 'Cheltenham Flyer', the fastest in the world, but over more than twice the distance.

On the press demonstration run of 27 September 1935, the new Gresley A4 No 2509 *Silver Link* twice hit 112mph, taking the world record away from the A3 *Papyrus*.

At one point during the inaugural run to Newcastle, Gresley squeezed through the corridor tender, tapped the driver on the shoulder and asked him to ease off a bit as they had twice touched 112mph and one of the LNER's more senior directors was showing signs of nerves! The driver had thought the speed was in the 90s.

The A4s were built initially in small batches, some for specific jobs. The first four were the silver ones for the 'Silver Jubilee', with 'silver' names. Then came a series for less specific duties, which carried apple green livery, and these were given bird names, perhaps an unfortunate departure from the racehorse tradition. A series of engines for the later 'Coronation' express was given garter blue livery, and names of countries in the Commonwealth.

The one real innovation on the A4s was the adoption of the Kylchap double blastpipe and chimney on the last few members of the class. It was this that gave No 4468 *Mallard* the ability to travel at 126mph to allow Gresley to make the headlines yet again in 1938.

The LMS was slow to catch up with the LNER, introducing Pacifics 10 years after Gresley's had first taken to the rails, but they were good and not only exceeded the power of Gresley's best, but gave them a run for their money in terms of speed too.

When the LNER's second streamlined train, the 'Coronation' was introduced, it brought the King's Cross to Edinburgh time down to six hours, with one stop, and narrowly beat the scheduled non-stop average speed of the 'Cheltenham Flyer'.

The LMS countered with its 'Coronation Scot' streamliner running between Euston and Glasgow. Again it was the press trip that broke the record; blue streamlined Stanier Pacific No 6220 *Coronation* reaching 114mph before having to brake (far too late) for Crewe station. Crewe took the speed record away from Doncaster, if only briefly.

In view of how close this train came to disaster, taking 25mph-restricted junctions and crossings at more than 70mph, a new gentlemen's agreement was entered into by the LMS and LNER to stop competing for record top speeds – at least not when carrying passengers.

Gresley still wanted to hold the record, though, and arranged some braking tests, on which the engine to be used was the fairly new but well run-in, double-chimneyed A4 No 4468 *Mallard*. Although the tests were to be conducted south of Peterborough, Gresley asked for the train to go north to Barkston Junction, to return down Stoke Bank, the line's fastest stretch of track. The officials on board were told at Grantham they would be trying for the record and were given the option of disembarking. None did, and No 4468 topped 126mph, setting a world steam speed record that has never been bettered.

Gresley had been awarded the CBE in WWI for his services to the war effort, and knighted in the King's Birthday Honours in 1936. In 1937, the 100th Gresley Pacific to be built, No 4498, was named *Sir Nigel Gresley* in a ceremony at Marylebone. The knighthood and the naming of an engine were two honours never previously bestowed on any railway chief mechanical engineer while in office.

The LNER served East Anglia, rural Lincolnshire, the north-east and eastern Scotland, none noted for its affluence. There was considerable coal traffic but this was in decline by the time the LNER was formed, and the LNER was possibly the least financially successful of the 'Big Four', but there are two points of view; perhaps the LNER should not have invested so heavily in the pursuit of speed records, or perhaps it makes its achievements all the more impressive.

Whatever the merits, by the middle of 1938, Doncaster had built not only the most-famous steam locomotive in the world, but also the fastest, and neither was ever to lose those titles.

Opposite top: The first: A4 Pacific No 2509 *Silver Link* is seen on a southbound 'Flying Scotsman' at Grantham. The silver A4s were no longer exclusively employed on the silver streamlined trains, and for the famous express to have paused at Grantham would have been unusual. COLOUR-RAIL

Opposite bottom: The 100th LNER Pacific; A4 No 4498, named after its designer *Sir Nigel Gresley*, pauses at Darlington. COLOUR-RAIL

Below: The fastest: A4 Pacific No 4468 *Mallard* near Potters Bar on 7 July 1938, the day of its record-breaking 126mph run down Stoke Bank. COLOUR-RAIL

Three A4 Pacifics line up at the National Railway Museum at York on 3 July 1988, the 50th anniversary of *Mallard's* 126mph run. Alongside No 4468 are No 4498 *Sir Nigel Gresley* and No 4464 *Bittern* masquerading as No 2509 *Silver Link*. BRIAN SHARPE

The A4 Pacifics were allocated to a relatively small number of depots, and this situation changed little until the class was phased out of ECML service. Doncaster was a shed only associated with A4s in pre-WWII days, so while all the class members would pass through with varying degrees of frequency, they comparatively rarely went 'on shed'. King's Cross, Grantham, Gateshead, and Haymarket (Edinburgh) were the long-term homes to most of the streamliners, generally staying at one shed for virtually the whole of their working lives.

They endured a certain amount of name changing. Some of the bird names were replaced by names of people, mainly LNER directors, while both apple green and silver were abandoned in favour of garter blue for all A4s, by which time war was imminent.

Thompson devised his somewhat more logical numbering system for the LNER, after a bit of a false start in 1946 and gave the numbers 1-34 to the surviving A4s, starting with the directors. The numbers although now sequential were still extremely haphazard and there was no attempt to number them in chronological order of building. The A4's later and more familiar BR numbers were dictated by Thompson's system and this is why the BR number sequence for the A4s bears virtually no relation to the LNER sequence.

The appearance of the A4s was altered during WWII when the valances over the driving wheels were removed to assist maintenance, but the engines were never completely de-streamlined. The class members re-acquired their garter blue livery after the war and BR experimented with various shades of blue for express engines after nationalisation. In 1950 though, GWR Brunswick green was adopted as standard for all BR express engines and the A4s quickly assumed this colour. As such they remained in charge of the most important ECML express workings until the first diesels arrived in 1958.

The A4s performances by the mid-1950s were comparable to the late 1930s in many respects, but circumstances had changed and BR was not trying to break records in terms of speed or endurance. The element of competition had reduced. Nevertheless, a

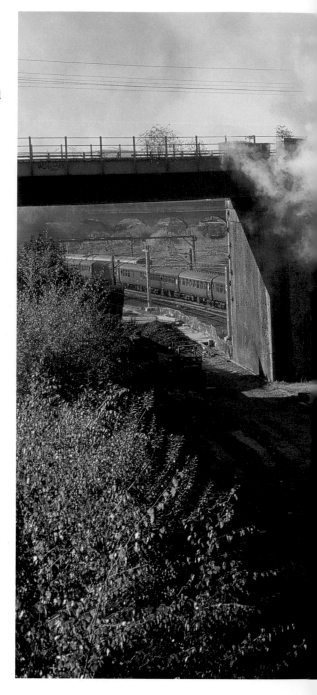

non-stop King's Cross to Edinburgh express was reintroduced, if only for a very short summer season, and the A4s worked this train until the last non-stop run of the 'Elizabethan' in 1961.

It is an A4, perhaps appropriately No 60007 *Sir Nigel Gresley* that holds the post-war British steam speed record, of 112mph down Stoke Bank in 1959.

It was six years after the appearance of the first diesels on ECML expresses, before the 'streaks' disappeared completely from the Doncaster railway scene. They lost all the top jobs to the Deltic diesels after 1961 but although many were scrapped in 1962-64, a surprising number moved to Scotland and found use on accelerated Glasgow to Aberdeen expresses for a few years as a result of the new diesels on this route being insufficiently reliable. This was undoubtedly the last significant chapter in the story of the achievements of 'The Plant's express steam locomotives. ∎

A4 Pacifics in order of construction, with LNER and BR numbers, and showing renaming

2509 60014 Silver Link	4492 60013 Dominion of New Zealand	4465 60020 Guillemot
2510 60015 Quicksilver	4493 60029 Woodcock	4466 60006 Herring Gull
2511 60016 Silver King	4494 60003 Osprey	Sir Ralph Wedgwood
2512 60017 Silver Fox	Andrew K McCosh	4467 60021 Wild Swan
4482 60023 Golden Eagle	4495 60030 Golden Fleece	4468 60022 Mallard
4483 60024 Kingfisher	4496 60008 Golden Shuttle	4499 60002 Pochard
4484 60025 Falcon	Dwight D Eisenhower	Sir Murrough Wilson
4485 60026 Kestrel/Miles Beevor	4497 60031 Golden Plover	4500 60001 Garganey
4486 60027 Merlin	4498 60007 Sir Nigel Gresley	Sir Ronald Matthews
4487 60028 Sea Eagle	4469 Gadwall/Sir Ralph Wedgwood	4900 60032 Gannet
Walter K Whigham	(scrapped after war damage)	4901 60005 Capercaillie
4488 60009 Union of South Africa	4462 60004 Great Snipe	Sir Charles Newton
4489 60010 Dominion of Canada	William Whitelaw	4902 60033 Seagull
4490 60011 Empire of India	4463 60018 Sparrow Hawk	4903 60034 Peregrine
4491 60012 Commonwealth of Australia	4464 60019 Bittern	Lord Faringdon

The V2s
Gresley's 2-6-2s

Most railways had their largest express engines, plus some smaller ones for less demanding passenger duties, then some medium-sized mixed-traffic engines, equally suitable for passenger and freight trains. The smaller passenger engines were often older express types displaced from the top jobs by newer and larger engines.

Gresley on the LNER did not follow this convention. He built his Pacifics, and used the Ivatt Atlantics and other inherited classes for other express work, and built some express 4-6-0s for the GE lines.

But for the mixed-traffic jobs, rather than go for smaller-wheeled 4-6-0s as the other companies did, he opted for a scaled-down Pacific, still with three cylinders, but with 6ft 2in as opposed to 6ft 8in driving wheels, and a 2-6-2 wheel arrangement. Classified V2, this design proved to be one of Gresley's greatest successes, yet it was the only class of 2-6-2 tender engine ever produced in Britain in any quantity.

It was said that they could do anything a Pacific could and they were credited with some prodigious feats of haulage especially during WWII. Three cylinders and small wheels gave them the power, and while they would not compete with Gresley's Pacifics for top speeds, the boiler never seemed to restrict their sustained steaming capacity in comparison with the A3s or A4s.

The V2s were put to work all over the LNER system, except East Anglia. Although Doncaster built the first five, the remainder were actually Darlington-built apart from two more short series of 10 engines each of which Doncaster produced.

'Green Arrow' had been the name of an LNER express goods service, and the first of the class took this name, following *Flying Scotsman's* lead in being named after a train. Only a handful of V2s were subsequently named, mostly on regimental/military lines.

A small number were fitted with Kylchap blastpipes and double chimneys, but this did not produce the economies which had been found with the A4s and A3s.

One of only 25 V2s were built at Doncaster. The first of the second batch, No 4843 *King's Own Yorkshire Light Infantry* is decorated for its naming ceremony at Doncaster in June 1939.
COLOUR-RAIL NE201

The V2's speciality was fast freight, which the class worked over the full length of the ECML between King's Cross and Aberdeen. The Great Central main line out of Marylebone was also classic V2 territory until the line was transferred to the London Midland Region in 1958. They were heavy engines and this precluded their use east of Cambridge, and on the West Highland route in Scotland.

Although Doncaster always had a substantial allocation of V2s, they did not last there until the end of steam at the Carr. A handful did however see out the end of steam at nearby York, No 60831 becoming the last of the class in service south of the border, withdrawn in December 1966.

Scotland was always home to many of the class, especially on the Edinburgh-Aberdeen route and the Waverley route to Carlisle, and it was No 60836 of Dundee Tay Bridge that became the last in regular service, also withdrawn at the very end of 1966, after hauling a farewell railtour over the Waverley route on 5 November. ■

Second World War

During both world wars 'The Plant' saw significant changes as the menfolk were called up to fight, and their girlfriends, wives, and daughters clocked on to tend the machines. Locomotive and carriage production was vital to the war effort but so too was munitions production. 'The Plant' therefore was adapted to produce war materials of all descriptions, from shells to Horsa gliders for the D-Day airborne assault. During WWII 'The Plant' became a target of German bombers and so air defence measures were introduced.

The war inevitably put a stop to the development of express steam locomotive design, with one notable exception. Gresley's one-time assistant, Oliver Bulleid took over as CME on the SR, and built his Pacifics. The Southern finally joined the big league despite it being wartime and Bulleid's Pacifics were very much derived from LNER ones, though radically different in appearance. In an indirect way, Doncaster's reputation for innovation did continue during the war, though not at Doncaster.

The SR's new Pacifics were real contenders for speed and power, but Bulleid's engines, although they tried to progress the art of steam locomotive design, were not ultimately successful in original form. In fact the successful part of their design, the overall dimensions, owed far more to Doncaster traditions than to either of the SR works which built them; Eastleigh and Brighton.

World War Two brought a stop to the competition between the 'Big Four', and ultimately to nationalisation, but which railway adapted best to the changing circumstances?

Dieselisation was still a long way in the future and wartime conditions seriously tested the steam locomotive engineering that had been developed in peacetime conditions of maintenance. Doncaster's engines, despite being some of the more refined forms of railway engineering, survived well and Gresley's V2s in particular, earned a reputation for feats of haulage undreamed of in peacetime.

But Edward Thompson came back on the scene when Gresley died in office in 1941, an imposter with a Darlington upbringing was in charge of locomotive design and production at Doncaster. It says a lot for the resilience of the workforce, that it adapted to a total change of philosophy, in the middle of wartime, and still retained its position as the LNER's number one workshop for locomotive building.

In a remarkable example of co-operation in pursuit of a common goal, Doncaster Works reluctantly built 50 LMS Stanier-designed 8F 2-8-0s during the War, and some of these ran in LNER service, classified O6. One, BR No 48518 is still in existence, although in derelict condition, its future at present uncertain. ∎

WD Austerity 2-8-0 No 90001 heads the breakdown crane through Doncaster in August 1961. The WD 2-8-0s were built to the design of Robert Riddles during the War, by North British and Vulcan Foundry. A substantial number were purchased by the LNER, and became an integral part of the railway scene around Doncaster right up to the end of steam.
COLOUR-RAIL BRE 2073

Thompson & Peppercorn A2 Pacifics

Right: LNER A2 Pacific No 60525 *AH Peppercorn* **on a southbound class E goods in 1959.** DAVID HOPPER

LNER A2/3 Pacific No 60523 *Sun Castle* **leaves Doncaster with an up express on 29 April 1962.** GAVIN MORRISON

A2 class Pacifics

	A2/3		60500 Edward Thompson	A2/3		60519 Honeyway
P2 2001	A2/2		60501 Cock o' the North	A2/3		60520 Owen Tudor
P2 2002	A2/2		60502 Earl Marischal	A2/3		60521 Watling Street
P2 2003	A2/2		60503 Lord President	A2/3		60522 Straight Deal
P2 2004	A2/2		60504 Mons Meg	A2/3		60523 Sun Castle
P2 2005	A2/2		60505 Thane of Fife	A2/3		60524 Herringbone
P2 2006	A2/2		60506 Wolf of Badenoch	A2		60525 AH Peppercorn
	A2/1	3696	60507 Highland Chieftain	A2		60526 Sugar Palm
	A2/1	3697	60508 Duke of Rothesay	A2		60527 Sun Chariot
	A2/1	3698	60509 Waverley	A2		60528 Tudor Minstrel
	A2/1	3699	60510 Robert the Bruce	A2		60529 Pearl Diver
	A2/3		60511 Airborne	A2		60530 Sayajirao
	A2/3		60512 Steady Aim	A2		60531 Bahram
	A2/3		60513 Dante	A2		60532 Blue Peter
	A2/3		60514 Chamossaire	A2		60533 Happy Night
	A2/3		60515 Sun Stream	A2		60534 Irish Elegance
	A2/3		60516 Hycilla	A2		60535 Hornet's Beauty
	A2/3		60517 Ocean Swell	A2		60536 Trimbush
	A2/3		60518 Tehran	A2		60537 Bachelor's Button
				A2		60538 Velocity
				A2		60539 Bronzino

Edward Thompson

Chief mechanical engineer of the LNER

Thompson's best-known design was the B1 4-6-0, but Doncaster played no part in building this substantial class. Preserved No 61264 leaves Scarborough with a railtour on 23 April 2005. BRIAN SHARPE

Two Gresley Pacifics were destroyed during the WWII; *Sir Ralph Wedgwood* by the Luftwaffe and *Great Northern* by Edward Thompson.

Gresley died in 1941, and it is said that his successor, the LNER's new chief mechanical engineer, Edward Thompson, tried to destroy everything Gresley had stood for. He had a dislike of Gresley's three-cylinder conjugated valve gear arrangement, and clearly felt that this was unsuitable for wartime conditions of reduced maintenance and tried to introduce a design of Pacific more suitable. In the event, wartime prevented him from really establishing this design.

Edward Thompson had briefly been carriage superintendent on the GNR, when Gresley became

locomotive superintendent, before moving to the North Eastern Railway, and was married to Sir Vincent Raven's daughter. He had never seen eye-to-eye with Gresley when they had worked together many years earlier.

Gresley's very 'hands-on' style of management disappeared when Thompson joined the LNER and another tier of management was introduced.

Rather than build a new express engine, Thompson rebuilt a Gresley one, but not just any Gresley engine, he butchered the original A1 Pacific No 4470 *Great Northern* itself, and what a mess he made of it!

The original NER-built A2s were now all withdrawn, only 10 original Gresley A1s were left, the rest either built new as A3s, or rebuilt as such, so Thompson designated the last remaining unrebuilt

Gresley A1s as A10s so he could call 'his' engine an A1. He also rebuilt Gresley's P2 2-8-2s as Pacifics with 6ft 2in as opposed to 6ft 8in driving wheels, and designated them as A2s.

Thompson's main disagreement with Gresley was over the conjugated valve gear. Thompson stuck with three cylinders for his express engines, but with three separate sets of valve gear. He was obsessed with the idea that all connecting rods must be the same length, rather than necessarily driving the same axle. The new *Great Northern* had its outside cylinders set well back on the frames but driving the middle driving wheels, while the middle cylinder drove the leading axle.

A rimless double chimney and a new and unfamiliar design of cab set off what was undoubtedly the ugliest Pacific ever seen within these shores,

despite being finished in royal blue with red lining. The LNER directors were said to have been quite vociferous in their disapproval. "It hasn't even got a proper chimney."

Thompson was not all bad, he may have lost his way with his express designs, but his mixed traffic B1 4-6-0 was just what the LNER needed, and Gresley had never produced a simple, straightforward medium-sized mixed traffic engine. Unfortunately, the tank version, the L1 2-6-4T was by comparison, useless, and never really outperformed the GNR N2 0-6-2Ts.

Thompson embarked on a programme of standardisation, simplification and rebuilding, using his B1 boiler on earlier classes such as the GCR O4 2-8-0 to produce numerous new classes and sub-classes. ∎

The Thompson rebuild of Gresley A1 Pacific No 4470 *Great Northern* as it first appeared from 'The Plant' in 1941.

A trainspotter reminisces

In late 1954 I made my first of many visits to Doncaster. Doncaster during the 1950s saw a good selection of motive power, and a wide range in the types of train workings. In addition to this was the lure of the locomotive works, referred to as the 'Plant', which brought a good variety of locomotives visiting the town, some types not usually seen there, going in and out of works and on running-in turns.

The aim was to arrive by 9am. Even by this time the four-wheeled station trolleys on the southern end of platform four could be crowded with schoolboy trainspotters, mostly dressed in short trousers and blazers. Essentials for the day were a notebook and pen or pencil, and an Ian Allan ABC book. Refreshments were usually sandwiches and a bottle of Tizer.

In steam days all stations were a hive of activity, with railway workers of all rank and file, going about their daily duties. Doncaster station was certainly busy during the 1950s, and in addition to the trains that stopped, started and terminated there, was the flow of through workings. The non-stop express passenger trains, referred to as 'Flyers', clattered through the station on the middle roads one after another behind gleaming Pacifics.

At this time the motive power for prestige trains was turned out in immaculately clean condition. If a dirty Pacific did turn up, it would probably be one running up the mileage to its next works overhaul. The highlights included 'The Elizabethan', worked in one direction by a Haymarket A4 Pacific, while a King's Cross one worked in the opposite direction on the balancing turn. Among other named trains were 'The Flying Scotsman', 'The White Rose' and 'The Yorkshire Pullman' which added interest to the procession of trains running in each direction.

In addition to the Pacifics were V2 2-6-2s. The speed limit through Doncaster was 60mph, and many of the expresses ran through at full speed, creating an awe-inspiring sight, while others suffered signal checks that reduced their speed, and even brought some to a brief standstill. There was also a good variety of engine types seen working trains that stopped, started or terminated at Doncaster, including B1, B16 and B17 4-6-0s, K2 and K3 2-6-0s, and D49 4-4-0s. Some of the stopping trains also attached or detached portions, adding to the interest, then there were trip-goods, pilot and empty stock workings, engines on which included J6 and JII 0-6-0s.

Tank engines included C13 4-4-2Ts, J50 0-6-0Ts and J52 0-6-0STs. In addition to these activities was a steady procession of heavy goods trains carrying coal, iron ore or steel. Engines on these included 02, 04 and WD 2-8-0s, joined by 9F 2-10-0s as the 1950s progressed. While lighter, faster goods trains carried fish or other perishables like fruit and vegetables, and engines on these included K3 2-6-0s and J39 0-6-0s. Fitting in between these goods trains were the express goods trains that were hauled by A1, A2, A3 and A4 Pacifics, and V2 2-6-2s.

The mid-1950s offered plenty of variety in coaching stock, with an abundance of ex-LNER stock, and even pre-Grouping stock, together with an increasing amount of British Railways Mk1 coaches. The liveries were crimson and cream for main line, and crimson for suburban stock, but some pre-BR stock was still in LNER livery. There was also an increasing amount of maroon-liveried coaching stock from late 1956.

From time to time we would abandon the station trolley to wander round the other platforms. We also made it a habit to visit the 'Plant' and engine shed. Going to these locations had to be fitted in so as to miss as few trains as possible, usually a quieter period in the day, referred to as 'the slack hour'. The usual practice was to go round the back of the 'Plant', then along the front to the paint shop and then down to the engine shed.

To get to the back of the 'Plant' required a walk out from the station and over the North Bridge then along the River Don bank. The fascination of this location was a line-up of what remained of some old C1 GNR Atlantics, being used as stationary boilers. From there we would walk back past the station, over Hexthorpe Road bridge and down the ramp to St James Bridge station, which had been retained to accommodate the many specials on race days. This gave an excellent view of activities, so made an ideal stopover on the way to the front of the 'Plant'.

The risk of what trains might be missed was weighed against what might be seen at the 'Plant'. Not that we ever had the chance to go inside and look round the various sections. We had to be content with whatever we could see from the outside. Our procedure was to go along the gennel that led past the paint shop, where a conveniently positioned old street lamp provided the chance to see through one of the paint shop windows. To accomplish this required a strenuous climb, gripping the lamp with the hands, while pushing against the concrete slab wall with the feet and inching one's way up to the lamp's crossbar below the lantern, and from this perch it was possible to see inside the paint shop. I must confess that this high vantage point was not always successfully reached on the first attempt.

One highlight well worth the effort of the climb on one occasion, stripped down ready for a repaint, was B17 4-6-0 No 61670 *City of London*. A little further along the perimeter wall there were cracks and small gaps between the concrete slabs that allowed a glimpse of anything in line with these spy-holes. Once back at St James Bridge we would enquire what had passed through during our absence.

Going down to the engine shed was less risky as the route was alongside the main line, and there were plenty of footholds in the side of the wall, so if a train was heard approaching it was possible to gain enough height to see it and get the locomotive's number. There was however a major distraction on the other side of the road, in the form of a well-stocked sweet shop that proved too big a lure to pass by without calling in to buy something. It was not unusual to miss a train while inside the shop, ogling the delights contained within the rows of sweet jars behind the counter.

Just beyond this point, where Balby Road bridge crossed the railway, our route veered left down to the shed. Shed visits yielded limited success, with many of the locomotives being out of sight and out of reach, but from time to time one would come along the

Doncaster became a magnet for many generations of trainspotters; **David Hopper** recalls days spent in the town in the 1950s.

LNER A1 Pacific No 60149 *Amadis* in 1959 with the 10.24am departure, the TThO Sunderland-King's Cross. DAVID HOPPER

turning triangle right at the side of our vantage point. This triangle was used until 1960, when it was abandoned after a turntable was installed. By chance on one occasion, I was invited to join a party about to go round the shed, once the permit holder had recruited the number of visitors specified on the document. The highlight of the tour was immaculate A2 Pacific No 60537 *Bachelors Button*, fresh from a works' overhaul and due to start running-in turns before going back north to the Scottish Region.

One of the special highlights of a Doncaster visit was the sight of a convoy of immaculate locomotives, referred to as the 'Plant Stream', fresh out of the works and making its way to the running shed. There could be up to half a dozen engines in the 'Plant Stream', some in steam, others not. A good place to watch it pass by was from the end of platform three, which extended further out than the others. One such convoy provided my first sighting of an N2 0-6-2T while another included the pioneer B17 No 61600 *Sandringham*, which really made the day. The B17s were referred to as 'Sandys', which was obviously derived from the pioneer's name.

The Pacifics always commanded attention, none more so than the streamlined A4s, whose passages were greeted with excited shouts of 'Streak, Streak!'. Often the call would go up even before the train came into view, sparked off by the distant moaning of a chime whistle that heralded the imminent approach of an A4. There was however another streamliner that wasn't an A4, but was certainly a big attraction. This was the W1 4-6-4 that had been rebuilt on similar lines to the A4s from the experimental No 10000, nicknamed the 'Hush Hush' through being built in great secrecy. In BR ownership it became No 60700.

The A3s had their own magic, as did the A1s and A2s. Both the latter types had smoke deflectors, referred to as 'Windshields', and the first one to recognise an A1 or A2 approaching would call out 'Wind Shielder', 'Winny' or 'Shielder'. Every so often a locomotive would come by that one or more in the group of trainspotters had not seen before, and a rousing cheer would ring out with shouts of 'Cop' amidst the noise and clatter of the passing train.

All these sights and sounds mingling with those of the station staff and train crews going about their work, added to the ambience of Doncaster station in steam days, while the staff seemed genuinely tolerant of having legions of schoolboys descending on the platforms.

The last four A4s were built with Kylchap double blastpipes and double chimneys, but the rest had single chimneys until being converted to the Kylchap system between May 1957 and November 1958. Single chimney A4s had a deep-throated roar similar to the A3s and V2s, which was strikingly different to the lighter whispery sound of Kylchap ones. Then between 1958 and 1960 the A3s were also converted to the Kylchap exhaust system, eliminating the sound of single chimney Gresley Pacifics. Although there were only four Kylchap-fitted A4s in the mid-1950s, the Kylchap sound was a very familiar one, as the A1s, many of the A2s, the W1 and A3 No 60097 *Humorist* also had the Kylchap system, the latter engine having been so fitted in 1937.

With a station as busy as Doncaster in the 1950s there was always the danger of being blocked-off, meaning a train being obscured from view behind another one on a nearer line. Obviously there were anxious moments when near misses occurred, with the offending train just clearing in time. My most memorable near miss involved a northbound fast goods that was slowly inching its way from St James bridge towards the station, running on caution signals, when another goods train running in the opposite direction, made up mostly of vans, rolled down platform four and drew to a standstill.

At this point the northbound goods got the road and the engine was opened up with some vigour, leaving me no option but to run along the platform and try to get beyond the back end of the standing goods. As the deep three-cylinder exhaust beat began to pick up, it became clear I would not achieve my goal, but by a fluke of good luck I drew alongside an open wagon, with seconds to spare before the hard-working engine roared past. It was the pioneer V2 2-6-2 No 60800 *Green Arrow*, resplendent in BR lined-black livery with the lion and wheel emblem.

During 1959, I made visits to Doncaster to take as many photographs as I could, but I had to be very selective in choosing which locomotives to photograph. One in particular that was a must, was immaculate A2 No 60525 *AH Peppercorn*, fresh from a works overhaul, which I photographed restarting from a signal check on the middle road through the station with a southbound class E express goods, during running-in turns before going back north to the Scottish Region. ■

Arthur Peppercorn

Chief mechanical engineer of the LNER

When Peppercorn took over after WWII, he effectively took the best parts of both Gresley's and Thompson's designs and came up with two designs of Pacific for the 1950s. Neither was meant to be as fast as Gresley's, but would be more economical, easier and cheaper to maintain, while theoretically producing more power. They were based on Thompson's experiments, but without some of Thomson's more dogmatic alterations, and while drawing on some of Gresley's stylistic features, looked more 1940s than 1920s while still being a balanced-looking engine, unlike Thompson's monstrosities.

The various A2 Pacifics were a hotch-potch, with little more in common with other class members than the 6ft 2in driving wheels. The A2/2 was the Thompson rebuild of Gresley's P2 2-8-2, the A2/1s were similar, but replaced an order for more V2s and incorporated parts such as the boiler. The A2/3s were new-build developments of the rebuilds, and the A2 itself was Peppercorn's later development of the design, and overall was much tidier in appearance. The A2 class itself, Nos 60525

Right: One of Peppercorn's most useful designs was the K1 2-6-0, built by North British after nationalisation. No 62005 is preserved and works on the North Yorkshire Moors Railway. BRIAN SHARPE

Below: Peppercorn A1 Pacific No 60131 *Osprey* on an up express at Doncaster station on 31 August 1961. GAVIN MORRISON

-39 was all built at Doncaster.

While the P2 rebuilds kept their Scottish names and the A2/1s continued that theme, the A2/3s and A2s continued the racehorse theme apart from No 500, the 2000th engine built at 'The Plant', and named *Edward Thompson* in honour of his retirement, and No 525, the first Peppercorn Pacific, the last Pacific to be built by the LNER and named after its designer, *AH Peppercorn*.

Peppercorn also built a mixed traffic 2-6-0, the K1, based on Thompson's two-cylinder rebuild of Gresley's K4 three-cylinder 2-6-0, which had already proved to be much more useful.

Depite its economic situation, and despite already having more Pacifics than any of the other railways,

the LNER was the only one of the 'Big Four' to design and start building new Pacifics after WWII. But again there are two points of view; did any railway really need more express steam engines, when surely more modern traction was to be the way forward; or was Doncaster once more ahead of the game?

The production A1 Pacifics were actually built under Peppercorn's jurisdiction and not until BR days. The naming policy was haphazard with further racehorses interspersed with names from LNER and pre-Grouping history, and later several on a Walter Scott theme. Nos 60114-60129 and 60153-60162 were built at Doncaster, the remainder at Darlington. ∎

A1 Pacifics

A1	60127 Wilson Worsdell		A1	60145 Saint Mungo		
A1	60128 Bongrace		A1	60146 Peregrine		
A1	60129 Guy Mannering		A1	60147 North Eastern		
A1	60130 Kestrel		A1	60148 Aboyeur		
A1/1 4470	60113 Great Northern	A1	60131 Osprey		A1	60149 Amadis
A1	60114 WP Allen	A1	60132 Marmion		A1	60150 Willbrook
A1	60115 Meg Merrillies	A1	60133 Pommern		A1	60151 Midlothian
A1	60116 Hal o' the Wynd	A1	60134 Foxhunter		A1	60152 Holyrood
A1	60117 Bois Roussel	A1	60135 Madge Wildfire		A1	60153 Flamboyant
A1	60118 Archibald Sturrock	A1	60136 Alcazar		A1	60154 Bon Accord
A1	60119 Patrick Stirling	A1	60137 Redgauntlet		A1	60155 Borderer
A1	60120 Kittiwake	A1	60138 Boswell		A1	60156 Great Central
A1	60121 Silurian	A1	60139 Sea Eagle		A1	60157 Great Eastern
A1	60122 Curlew	A1	60140 Balmoral		A1	60158 Aberdonian
A1	60123 HA Ivatt	A1	60141 Abbottsford		A1	60159 Bonnie Dundee
A1	60124 Kenilworth	A1	60142 Edward Fletcher		A1	60160 Auld Reekie
A1	60125 Scottish Union	A1	60143 Sir Walter Scott		A1	60161 North British
A1	60126 Sir Vincent Raven	A1	60144 King's Courier		A1	60162 Saint Johnstoun

Above: A1 Pacific No 60136 *Alcazar*, with a down Newcastle express, leaves Doncaster in April 1962.
COLOUR-RAIL BRE 1930

Left: A1 Pacific No 60149 *Amadis* shunts the Hull portion of a King's Cross express at Doncaster on 24 March 1962. GAVIN MORRISON

Right: LNER A1 Pacific No 60119 *Patrick Stirling* restarts from a signal check at Doncaster with an up Class C express goods in 1959.
DAVID HOPPER

Doncaster's Railway Legends

Diesel shunters

In very presentable condition, Class 09 350hp 0-6-0 diesel shunter No 09106 shunts at Doncaster in 2007. Formerly D3927, then 08759, it was actually built at Horwich in 1961 for the Scottish Region.
BRIAN SHARPE

I t was a long time before diesel engines became practicable for propulsion of main line trains, despite the fact that the US and many other countries worldwide were embracing diesel traction quite successfully.

In the 1930s though, it was realised that a small diesel engine deployed in an 0-4-0 or 0-6-0 shunting locomotive, was certainly practicable, and shunting was just the environment where diesel traction really scored. All of the Big Four started building diesel shunters, and the LNER was no exception, although it actually built only four. They were built at Doncaster largely following the design that was already in service on the LMS.

Even Britain's private locomotive building industry saw serious orders to be gained and several made the change from steam to diesel production.

All four companies experimented with new forms of traction, and possibly the LMS was most advanced with dieselisation, but it was Derby which spearheaded this development initially, not Crewe.

When BR finally rushed headlong into its modernisation programme from 1955, Doncaster seriously missed out. All it was nominated to build were some 204hp diesel shunters, admittedly 82 of them, plus just 23 350hp 0-6-0s. Quite a kick in the teeth for one of the most respected railway workshops in the world, but at least Doncaster could concentrate on getting the best out of its steam products for a few more years.

The smaller design of 0-6-0 diesel shunter was phased out by 1990, although many still exist. The 350hp machines though are still in service on the national network, although now in very small numbers, as shunting is now becoming a thing of the past.

'The Plant' did little diesel locomotive construction,

Above: Class 03 D2112 was one of many of the class to be privately preserved, but this Doncaster-built example has returned to commercial freight traffic and regularly hauls heavy stone trains on the Boston Docks' branch, passing classic GNR lineside infrastructure.
BRIAN SHARPE

Above left: Doncaster-built Class 03 diesel shunters Nos 2065 and 2093 inside the now-preserved Barrow Hill Roundhouse on 11 June 1972.
BRIAN SHARPE

but it was heavily involved in testing new designs for general acceptance by BR. In 1965, a new diesel locomotive test house was built east of the Crimpsall shop. Carriage construction and major repairs ceased and light wagon repairs were moved back to 'The Plant' from the Carr. ∎

'The Plant's electrics

While the LNER was not in the premier league for early experimentation with diesel traction, it inherited an appetite for electrification from one of its constituents, the NER. This company had electrified the Tyneside suburban routes in 1909, plus the Newcastle Quayside branch for freight traffic, then moved on to the Shildon–Newport line using big electric locomotives for hauling heavy coal traffic. It even thought seriously about electrifying its part of the ECML. Although falling traffic levels and the need for expensive equipment renewal had led to the Shildon route being de-electrified in 1934, the LNER was already sufficiently impressed that it set out to electrify the GCR Trans-Pennine Woodhead route at 1500Vv DC overhead.

Gresley was involved in the development of the prototype design of locomotive for the route, a Bo-Bo, No 6701 which was built at Doncaster in 1941. It was trialled on the Manchester to Altrincham suburban line, but the outbreak of war brought the project to a halt. After the war No 6701 was sent to Holland where it ran for several years, while the old GCR route across the Pennines was electrified. The prototype engine, now numbered 26000 and named *Tommy*, was joined by 57 others built at the former GCR Gorton works in Manchester, plus seven of a larger Co-Co design. The project was completed in 1954, including the construction of new larger bore tunnels.

The wires were eventually to extend to Wath yard and to Rotherwood sidings, both well to the east of Sheffield and not far from Doncaster. It is perhaps surprising that the opportunity was not taken to extend the wires into the huge yards at Doncaster, but coal traffic flowed in a set pattern established over many years and following the precedents set by the pre-Grouping companies. Coal flowed from south Yorkshire through Doncaster and on to London, or through Doncaster to Humberside, or across the Pennines to Lancashire or to Liverpool for export, depending on whether the pit happened to have been served by the GNR or GCR, but it was not generally moved from Doncaster to Lancashire.

The Woodhead electrification was successful, and at the same time, the first of the Liverpool Street suburban lines was electrified on the same system. However it had taken a long time because of the war and technology had moved on. Future main line electrification would be at 25kV ac, not 1500V dc.

The decimation of freight traffic, and coal in particular made the line across the Pennines superfluous and it closed in 1982. The Manchester end with its suburban traffic, as well as the Liverpool Street lines, were converted to 25kV by BR. Nevertheless, Doncaster had built the first locomotive for the first successful overhead electric inter-city passenger and freight route in Britain. ∎

Above: Class 305/2 electric-multiple-unit No 305503 arrives at Liverpool Street in September 1979. The Great Eastern inner-suburban electrification was started by the LNER in the 1940s but but suspended during WW2. The original units were built by Metropolitan-Cammell and Birmingham Railway Carriage & Wagon Co under the supervision of AH Peppercorn, and entered service from 1949. The units were converted to 25kV ac operation in 1959-61, and electrification of GE suburban services was extended. New EMU stock introduced at this time included 19 of these four-car Class 305/2 units which were built at 'The Plant' in Doncaster.
FRED KERR

Left: Gresley pre-Nationalisation designed EM1 (Class 76) Bo-Bo electric No 76037 appropriately heads a train of pre-Nationalisation carriages, of Great Western origin near Dinting on the Woodhead route on 21 April 1979.
BRIAN SHARPE

British Railways

Nationalisation had little immediate effect on the great locomotive works as rationalisation had already taken place under the 'Big Four' companies and for many years, things carried on much as before, with largely the same workshops responsible for building engines. Doncaster started on Peppercorn's A1 and A2 Pacifics, and simply carried on building some of these these designs. An indication of future direction, though, was that Doncaster built some LMS 4F 2-6-0s, designed by the last CME of the LMS, HG Ivatt, son of HA Ivatt of GNR fame.

An important step for the newly formed British Railways, was to come up with its own designs of locomotives suitable for use throughout the system. This may not in fact have been wise as different designs suited different parts of the country,

LNER A2 Pacific No 60526 *Sugar Palm* and A3 No 60035 *Windsor Lad* inside Doncaster works in January 1959. GAVIN MORRISON

particularly with regard to varying quality of coal. It would also have been preferable to push ahead faster with the early trials of more modern traction which the various 'Big Four' companies had dabbled in.

Nevertheless, the famous 1948 Locomotive Exchanges took place to finally prove once and for all, which company's engines were best. So Doncaster saw a GWR King, an LMS Duchess and a Bulleid Pacific, among other foreign types, passing through. As Peppercorn's A1s had not yet entered service, Gresley's streamlined A4s were chosen to represent the old LNER.

The trials were largely inconclusive as all the tested engines were good, but not always directly comparable, and steam engines rarely perform at their best away from home. The A4s had a couple of unfortunate failures on test, but with LMS men, including Robert Riddles in charge of design, pre-war Gresley-style three-cylinder propulsion with conjugated valve gear was never going to find favour.

Another major change was to be in the appearance of the trains. New liveries were tried, and it was a couple of years before things really settled down in this respect. A coach livery of carmine and cream was quickly adopted by most regions, while to begin with engines continued to be painted in pre-nationalisation colours, but with 'British Railways' on the tender, and eventually a number in the new BR series. This involved adding 60,000 to all LNER engine numbers, and a smokebox numberplate was adopted as

'The Plant's last steam engine, BR Standard 4MT 2-6-0 No 76114 at Doncaster in October 1957. COLOUR-RAIL BRE 1631

standard. This was an LMS tradition never used by the other three companies.

Goods engines remained black, engines used on passenger services had LNWR style lining and express engines were blue with black and white lining. GWR Brunswick green was applied haphazardly to engines which were not really mixed traffic, but not express either, so for example V2 2-6-2s carried mixed-traffic lined black livery. Apple-green engines, and teak-liveried coaches disappeared from the Doncaster railway scene. Blue was abandoned in favour

of Brunswick green for express engines, and from 1957, Brunswick green was applied to a greater number of classes, V2s included, while LMS maroon became standard coach livery.

The Western Region then adopted chocolate and cream for coaches and the Southern Region malachite green. The Eastern Region considered varnished teak, even for steel coaches, as in later LNER days but went with maroon along with the London Midland, North Eastern and Scottish regions. ■

Un-named LNER A1 Pacific No 60114 on display at Doncaster works in 1948 in BR apple green livery.
COLOUR-RAIL BRE 1422

BR Standard steam locomotives

In 1948, Doncaster was still up in the top three of British locomotive workshops, but was slipping, having had little involvement in new traction, while the LMS at Crewe/Derby, had two main line diesels, and the GWR at Swindon was trying out a gas-turbine locomotive.

There was still a strong vested interest in steam though, and in 1951 BR introduced the first of 999 steam engines to be built to the design of its CME, Robert Riddles. He was an LMS man, and although he was prepared to look at features from the other three of the 'Big Four', LMS traditions would inevitably predominate. Forget three cylinders, and conjugated valve gear was already long gone out of favour.

The new BR designs, were simple, with two cylinders, although there were no Class 8 express engines involved – at first.

All of the major workshops were involved in the design, but each concentrated on small parts of the overall design of a particular class. Doncaster did coupling and connecting rods, valve gear and some cylinder details. Construction of the various

locomotives was then allocated to workshops according to their capacity at the time.

Brighton, Derby, Crewe, Doncaster and Swindon were the workshops which shared the building of the BR Standard classes, but Doncaster's contribution was relatively small, just a batch of 42 Class 5 4-6-0s in 1955-57, 10 Class 4 2-6-4Ts and 80 of the 115 Class 3 2-6-0s from 1952, finishing with No 76114 in 1957, the last of 2228 steam locomotives to be built at Doncaster.

The BR Standards never found much favour on the Eastern Region, with the exception of the superb 9F 2-10-0s which took over the heaviest GN main line coal trains.

For reasons which are not quite clear though, one 8P Pacific was built by BR in 1954, and although built at Crewe, it had three cylinders, in best Doncaster traditions. It is even said that No 71000 *Duke of Gloucester's* dimensions owed more to Doncaster practice than Crewe's, so perhaps Doncaster contributed more than is generally realised to Britain's last express steam locomotive. ■

The End of Steam

In 1957, the last of more than 2000 steam locomotives was built and, in 1962, carriage building finished. 'The Plant' continued however with the works being modernised and seeing the addition of a diesel locomotive repair shop. Under British Rail Engineering Limited (BREL), new diesel shunters and 25kV electric locomotives were built, plus, since 1976, Class 56 and Class 58 diesel-electric locomotives.

In fact, production of main line diesel locomotives, when it commenced in the late 1950s, was not primarily at the major established centres. Swindon built some, as did Crewe eventually, and Derby built more than most BR workshops. Private contractors, particularly English Electric and Brush, built many diesels but Newton-le-Willows and Loughborough, despite their proud records of engineering

achievement, never attained the legendary status of Crewe or Doncaster.

However, Doncaster simply did not build diesels, at least not main line ones, and undoubtedly loses points as a result, even against its old rival Darlington. The Eastern Region though, was at the forefront of the dieselisation process and took responsibility for testing new locomotives built elsewhere, so Doncaster did play an important part, while still maintaining its now-quite old steam fleet in tip-top condition.

Doncaster probably received the ultimate accolade in this period when one particular class of diesels, the North British Type 2s were found to be so unsatisfactory that they were replaced by steam engines, Doncaster-built ones, working on part of the West Coast Main Line, from Glasgow to Aberdeen, traditionally part of the Crewe empire.

Cynics might say that the situation was partly Doncaster's fault, as the first 10 of the North British diesels had been thoroughly tested there and found to be satisfactory. On the Eastern Region no less, under the eyes of Doncaster engineers.

As a result of the unreliability of the North British diesels, several Gresley A4 Pacifics, redundant from ECML workings, went to Scotland to replace the diesels for several years on the Glasgow -Aberdeen expresses on the one-time LMS line.

Doncaster appeared to take a back seat through much of the modernisation process, but was heavily involved, despite not actually building new main line diesels. Diesels took over the express workings through the town between 1958 and 1963, mostly English Electric or Brush products. Diesel Multiple Units took over local services during the same period and there were line closures and reductions in services, although Doncaster did not suffer too badly.

'The Plant' completed the overhaul of its last steam engine on 6 November 1963, Scottish Region A4 Pacific No 60009 *Union of South Africa*.

The LNER Pacifics gradually retreated northwards as dieselisation took hold. A surprising change in the last few years of steam was the virtual abandonment of the Grantham and York locomotive changes with the double-chimneyed A3s as well as A4s starting to make much longer journeys away from home. Steam ended at King's Cross in May 1963, and was theoretically banned south of Peterborough.

By the end of 1964, steam ended at Peterborough, leaving no A3s in service south of the border. Gateshead's last A4s were either withdrawn or transferred to Scotland by the end of 1964, so the appearance of any LNER Pacific in Doncaster after the beginning of 1965 would have been extremely rare.

The last LNER Pacifics on the books in England were a couple of A1s in the north-east, Nos 60124 *Kenilworth* and 60145 *Saint Mungo*, but once they were withdrawn, in March/April 1966, an era had ended as no longer would an LNER Pacific be seen on the main line through Doncaster – with one exception of course.

Even the heavy coal traffic, which remained predominantly steam-worked until 1965, was quickly dieselised when the Eastern Region's remaining steam working was eliminated in one fell swoop. Doncaster shed lost its steam allocation on 23 April 1966.

The last steam locomotives allocated to Doncaster were:
LNER B1 4-6-0s: 61042, 61121, 61158, 61250, 61329, 61360, 61406
GCR O4 2-8-0s: 63653, 63781, 63785, 63818, 63858
WD Austerity 2-8-0s: 90001, 90002, 90013, 90018, 90037, 90063, 90075, 90148, 90154, 90156, 90369,

90410, 90437, 90471, 90538, 90551, 90636, 90675, 90709
BR Standard 9F 2-10-0s: 92182, 92183, 92201

Interestingly all four classes at the end were types with which Doncaster was never involved in the construction of. Even the Great Central heavy freight 2-8-0s had outlived the locally built Great Northern ones.

With Leeds sheds retaining steam until the end of September 1967, Doncaster still saw isolated steam workings up until that date, although mainly by LMS types. ∎

Above: Pioneer A4 Pacific No 60014 *Silver Link*. Incredibly it was scrapped at Doncaster shortly after this photograph was taken on 3 February 1963. GAVIN MORRISON

Below: Wakefield shed's LMS Jubilee 4-6-0 No 45739 *Ulster* with a parcels train at Doncaster in November 1966. COLOUR-RAIL

Deltics –
but not built at Doncaster

One type of diesel came to epitomise the East Coast Main Line in the years immediately following the end of steam. It was a class of engine worthy of assuming the mantle of the renowned Gresley streamlined Pacifics. It would make the story of Doncaster's continuing pursuit of excellence complete if 'The Plant' had built the Deltics, but unfortunately it did not.

English Electric, across the Pennines at Newton-le-Willows was the leading manufacturer of diesel locomotives, both for BR and abroad. In fact the company was a little frustrated at BR's lack of commitment to modernisation, and when it built the first Deltic, which was first contemplated in the 1940s, it was intended as a demonstrator locomotive for overseas orders. It was fitted with a large headlight with a view to securing orders from the US.

Initially though, BR gave English Electric the opportunity to prove itself on express services in Britain, before it had placed any orders for new diesels. Although the big blue Deltic started on the West Coast Main Line out of Euston, BR quickly committed itself to electrification of that route and *Deltic* moved to the Eastern Region.

The LMS had ordered two 1500hp diesels, and the SR three of 1750hp, the third one uprated to 2000hp. Fifteen-hundred horse-power was the equivalent of a mixed-traffic Class 5 4-6-0, and both LMS diesels were needed to keep time on an express. Deltic, using a Napier power unit developed for marine applications, offered 3300hp, and was every bit the equal of a Class 8 Pacific.

Above: No 55008 *The Green Howards* **departs from Doncaster with a down express on 20 May 1978.**
BRIAN SHARPE

Above left: Deltic No 55010 *King's Own Scottish Borderer* **heads south out of Doncaster past Bridge Junction on 21 April 1976.**
BRIAN SHARPE

Left: The Deltics were not built at Doncaster but 'The Plant' maintained them, and eventually scrapped most of them. To mark the end of the class in BR service, the last survivors were gathered together in Doncaster Works' yard for a public open day on 27 February 1982. Nos 55009 *Alycidon* **and 55019** *Royal Highland Fusilier* **were subsequently bought for preservation by the Deltic Preservation Society, which maintains them at a purpose-built shed at Barrow Hill Roundhouse, Staveley.** BRIAN SHARPE

It had a few years of trials in the 1950s and the ER management was impressed. Twenty-two were ordered and were delivered during 1961. The Deltics were a success from the start, and basically replaced the 34 A4 Pacifics. In an ideal world, more would have been built to replace all the LNER Pacifics, but the Deltics were expensive diesels, and with 2500hp and 2750hp machines becoming available which would be more economical to operate, the decision was taken not to order more Deltics.

Heavy maintenance of the fleet was undertaken at 'The Plant', and so the Deltics, with their distinctive drone, were to have a long association with Doncaster, which ended with most of the fleet being scrapped there, following their displacement by High-Speed Trains in 1978-81.

Happily, no fewer than six have been preserved and some have seen main line activity, occasionally seen roaring through Doncaster on the through roads, almost like the old days. ■

Left: February 1982 was not the end of the Deltics. No 55002 *King's Own Yorkshire Light Infantry*, already returned to two-tone green livery, was destined for the National Collection and travelled under its own power to the National Railway Museum at York later that afternoon. No 55016 *Gordon Highlander* was later purchased by Deltic 9000 Ltd as a source of spare parts for D9000 *Royal Scots Grey*, but later returned to service in its own right.
BRIAN SHARPE

Class 71 Southern Region electrics

Although Doncaster did not build main line diesels until much later, it did build significant batches of electrics. The Southern Railway had electrified much of its route mileage, mainly for multiple-unit operation on suburban trains, but did design some main line electric locomotives. In fact Sir Nigel Gresley's one-time assistant, Oliver Bulleid took over the responsibility for building the first two engines when he joined the SR. They were designed to operate on both third-rail, and overhead wire electrified lines.

It was much later, when BR's modernisation plan was getting into full swing, that the Southern Region ordered 20 more electric locomotives, which were a lighter, more refined version, and the order went to Doncaster, the first, E5000, appearing in 1958.

Electrics were used on freight traffic between London and the Kent coast, and prestige expresses such as the 'Golden Arrow' and 'Night Ferry'. In the 1960s, 10 were rebuilt as electro-diesels, for use on the Bournemouth line, but this extensive rebuilding took place at Crewe. Nevertheless, as traffic patterns changed, both the original (Class 71) and rebuilt (Class 74) engines became redundant and were withdrawn by 1977.

One, E5001 was secured by the National Railway Museum, and was restored to original condition by BREL at Doncaster. ■

Class 85 West Coast electrics

Five different classes of 25kV AC electric locomotives were built for comparative evaluation in service on BR's showpiece electrified West Coast Main Line. All basically similar, they had bodyshells, electrical equipment and traction equipment supplied by several different manufacturers. The AL1 to AL5, later Classes 81 to 85, monopolised WCML services while the route was being electrified in the early 1960s.

BR's plan was to electrify the WCML throughout, then immediately move on to the East Coast Main Line. 'The Plant' therefore became involved, by building the second batch of AL5s, intended for ECML service, but initially to be loaned to the London Midland Region. In fact this was the only class built by BR workshops, with AEI/ English Electric acting as subcontractor.

It was government interference that put the electrification of the northern end of the WCML, and the ECML electrification on hold indefinitely, and the Class 85s never did return to the Eastern Region. ■

Class 86 West Coast electrics

After an evaluation period five early classes of electric locomotives on the WCML, had the best features of each combined into a standard design, the AL6, the first of which entered service in 1965. A hundred of these were required, and production was shared between 'The Plant' at Doncaster, and English Electric's Vulcan Foundry, E3101 to E3140 being Doncaster's batch.

The AL6s became standard motive power for WCML expresses after the end of steam; diesels only having been used on a temporary basis. While the ECML Pacifics were succeeded by the Deltics, which could at least be considered worthy and distinctive successors, the Stanier Pacifics on the WCML handed over to what was, in comparison, a very plain box on wheels.

Nevertheless they were powerful and reliable engines, and for many years, products of 'The Plant' helped to keep the wheels turning on the rival West Coast route.

Known as Class 86 under the TOPS system, the class also inaugurated electric operations on the GE main line between Liverpool Street and Norwich, and engines of the class have occasionally been seen on specials passing through Doncaster, since electrification of the ECML. Although no longer in regular timetabled passenger service, several remain in use on Freightliner trains. ■

Left: A Class 86 made redundant from WCML services, approaches Stowmarket on the Great Eastern main line. BRIAN SHARPE

Class 56
Type 5 heavy freight diesels

Above: On 28 May 2007, Jarvis Fastline Class 56 No 56303 heads a railtour into Stainforth & Hatfield to the north-east of Doncaster where the West Riding and Grimsby avoiding line to the north meets the MSLR line towards Cleethorpes. BRIAN SHARPE

'The Plant' completed the overhaul of its last steam engine in 1963, and settled into a routine of maintaining part of BR's diesel locomotive fleet. An upturn in its fortunes came in 1977, when new Type 5 heavy freight diesels were being built, and although a product of Brush Traction in Loughborough, building was subcontracted to a company in Romania. The Class 56 Co-Cos were designed by Brush to BR's specifications, using a 3250hp Ruston Paxman engine, and initially destined for MGR coal trains in the Eastern Region. Brush did not have the capacity to build them and assembly was sub-contracted to Electroputiere in Romania. The engines when they arrived, were not found to be altogether satisfactory, and Doncaster was hastily asked to take over part of the order. 'The Plant' built some big diesels at last, although the last 30 of the order were built at Crewe.

When diesels were first introduced, they tended to be designed using the criteria of mixed-traffic steam engines. Few were really dedicated express engines apart from the Deltics, which were the only Type 5 (more than 3000hp) for many years. For freight service, most classes were found to be adequate, and earlier designs tended to be demoted to freight traffic as newer designs were introduced.

However, the patterns of freight traffic changed dramatically as pick up goods and extensive remarshalling of trains was abandoned in favour of block loads, especially of coal, and specialised high-powered types such as the Class 56 developed from these changes.

The sphere of operation for the Class 56s gradually widened, but the class was frequently demoted to menial engineers' train duties and in 2005 the last ones were withdrawn. Most have not been scrapped though; one or two entered preservation, three are back in main line service with Jarvis Fastline, based in Doncaster, and others could see further use, in Britain or perhaps even abroad. ∎

Left: In Railfreight grey livery, Class 56 No 56079 passes Barrow Hill with a typical East Midlands' coal train. BRIAN SHARPE

Inset:Doncaster 86 No 56057 *British Fuels* was the first Class 56 to operate in preservation, but has since been sold, for further main line service. BRIAN SHARPE

Class 58
Type 5 heavy freight diesels

The Class 56 was never one of Britain's best diesel designs, but Doncaster cannot be blamed for that. The works continued by building the Class 58s, another Type 5 freight engine, which if not very exciting, proved to be quite satisfactory in service.

The Class 58 that quickly followed the Class 56 was very different looking in design. Even though BREL had ended up building the Class 56, which was essentially a Brush design, it had also pressed ahead with its own radically different design, using a similar 3300hp Ruston Paxman engine.

The Class 58s were of modular construction with all the weight carried on a girder rather than by the bodywork, and it was hoped the design would lead to export orders.

The sphere of operation of the Class 58s, though, was much more limited than the Class 56s, all 50 being based at Toton, near Nottingham, for local coal traffic and longer runs to various power stations such as Didcot, plus flyash trains to the ER.

The class was significant in that it brought to an end the long period of corporate rail blue livery by appearing in a striking grey, yellow and red livery, with the BR double arrow symbol taking the full height of the bodyside. A 'Railfreight' logo adorned the cabside and heralded a change to BR's structure, with freight and passenger operations being increasingly separated.

Only one more class of conventional diesel locomotive was ever built in Britain after the Class 58s, and the Brush Class 60 was never considered a great success, so maybe Doncaster should be credited with building Britain's last successful new diesels.

Although a useful design and nowhere near life-expired, the Class 58 was already being phased out as coal traffic contracted, and the arrival of EWS's American Class 66s to a similar specification soon spelled the end for the Class 58s. Some survive, though, and have seen service on the continent. No 58001 was restored to original livery by EWS, and No 58050 has been designated for the National Collection. ■

Class 58s Nos 58012, 58013 and 58014 being under construction by BREL at Doncaster on 31 October 1983. GAVIN MORRISON

Left: The first of the class, No 58001, is handed over to BR in a ceremony at Doncaster on 9 December 1982. GAVIN MORRISON

Below: The two Doncaster-built Type 5 diesel classes join forces as Class 58 No 58044 and Class 56 No 56097 head a flyash train through Peterborough on 16 October 1987. BRIAN SHARPE

Open Days
A look behind the scenes

A4 Pacific No 4468 *Mallard*
rightly takes pride of place at
the 1978 Railex 125 event.
DAVID HOPPER

A large part of enthusiast folklore in steam days, revolved around locomotive sheds and their relative ease of access or otherwise. You could collect a lot of numbers by hanging around on station platforms or bridges, but it was so much more productive if you could get into a shed, and get out again before the foreman saw you.

However, railway locomotive works though were a different matter. They had real security and you did not enter without official permission, usually as part of an organised tour.

There was always a fascination about the places, not just with trainspotters and enthusiasts, but with the public at large. Many locomotive workshops opened their doors on occasions so the public could see locomotives in the course of being built, and under heavy overhaul.

Doncaster was no exception, and on occasions, some major exhibitions of railway hardware have been staged at 'The Plant'.

Since the end of steam, there have been events at 'The Plant' such as the *Blue Peter* naming in 1971, Railex 125 in 1978, the Deltic farewell of 1982 and Doncaster 150 in 2003. ■

The National Railway Museum's Stirling Single No 1 and GNR Atlantics No 990 *Henry Oakley* and No 251 on display at the 125th anniversary open day at Doncaster Works in 1978. MORTONS ARCHIVES

En route to the 1978 event, A3 Pacific No 4472 *Flying Scotsman* called at Keighley to collect GNR Atlantic No 990 *Henry Oakley*. The short train passes Goosehill Junction, Normanton. BRIAN SHARPE

RAILEX 125

An Open Weekend to celebrate the 125th Anniversary of British Rail Engineering Limited's Doncaster Works

17th & 18th JUNE 1978

Souvenir Programme   20p

East Coast Main Line Electrification

Electrification was thought of as a viable alternative to steam in the early years of the 20th century, but early experiments were mainly confined to busy suburban routes operated by multiple-unit trains, The North Eastern Railway was a leader in this field, electrifying its North Tyneside suburban routes, plus the short Quayside branch near Newcastle for freight traffic. Much more ambitious was the Shildon to Teesside route for heavy coal traffic, and the NER was giving serious thought to following this with electrification of its portion of the ECML.

While this did not happen, the LNER pressed ahead with a scheme to electrify the Manchester – Sheffield line, on similar principles, but by the time it was completed 1500V dc was obsolete technology.

British Railways committed itself to its first major

main line electrification project at 25kV ac. Euston to Birmingham, Crewe, Manchester and Liverpool was Britain's busiest main line and an obvious candidate, but it turned out to be such an expensive project that it would be many years before any further routes could be considered. A continuation onwards to Carlisle and Glasgow was originally envisaged, to be immediately followed by the ECML, but north of Crewe had to wait nearly ten years until 1974 and it was more than ten years after that before the ECML's turn came for the wires.

This started earlier with suburban lines from King's Cross as far as Cambridge and Peterborough, while Leeds to Skipton also saw wires erected. The current was energized as far as Doncaster in the summer of 1988 and completed through to Edinburgh in 1990.

The Deltics were long gone and HSTs or IC125s held the fort almost exclusively by then. The new trains for the ECML were dubbed IC225 (kph) or 140mph, although they have never done this in regular service.

Doncaster had little involvement in the building of the new trains, just as it had not built the Deltics, any of the other ECML diesels, or the HST sets, although it had built some electrics for the West Coast.

Crewe built the Class 91s, and these have proved to be the last main line locomotives to be built in Britain. Since 1988, new passenger trains have always been multiple-unit designs, while the freight sector has been buying from America.

A major civil engineering task undertaken shortly before electrification was the Selby diversion, a few miles to the north of Doncaster. New coal mining operations north of Selby were threatening to literally undermine the ECML, and underground subsidence threatened to severely restrict speeds on the line. A new line was built, diverging from the one-time York & North Midland, at Colton Junction, south of York, and running west of Selby, to rejoin the NER main line at Temple Hirst Junction. This had the added bonus of bypassing the Selby swing bridge with its severe speed restriction.

The NER line was closed completely between Selby and Chaloners Whin Junction at York, and ECML expresses now took their third different route in 150 years between Doncaster and York. ■

Brush-built prototype Class 89 electric No 89001 *Avocet* arrives at Doncaster with the first passenger-carrying electrically-hauled train to the town, the Mallard 50th anniversary special from King's Cross which would be taken over by the record-breaking A4 Pacific.
BRIAN SHARPE

No 1
The Stirling Single

The 50th locomotive built at Doncaster was the first of Patrick Stirling's legendary 8ft Singles. Under Stirling's rule, GNR locomotive numbering was haphazard, and new engines took the next available number, sometimes from one recently withdrawn. The first five took the numbers 1, 8, 33, 2 and 3, the last of the class being No 778. They were built in pairs, only the two engines in a pair actually being identical. No doubt Stirling pulled some strings to get the original No 1 withdrawn so that the number became available for his flagship design.

No 1 was the first of Doncaster's steam locomotives to be preserved; the first of what was to be a reasonably representative selection by the end of steam, but in comparison with other railways, the LNER and its constituents fared very badly in terms of numbers of preserved steam engines.

However, No 1 also became one of the first preserved steam engines to be steamed again many years after withdrawal, and this set the scene for what was to follow, as Doncaster-built engines played an active role in the story of steam preservation.

The engine was not scrapped on withdrawal in 1907, but was cleaned up and put on display at an exhibition at Wembley in 1909. After that it moved to King's Cross shed where it remained in store for a while before moving back to 'The Plant' at Doncaster, where it languished in the old varnish shop for a few years. Nevertheless it remained safe, and it is said that Gresley himself kept a protective eye on it.

Other railway companies 'preserved' engines in much the same way but then cut them up because they were in the way, or the steel was needed. Several

historic engines disappeared in this way during the two world wars.

No 1 though came in for special treatment, and was given a brand-new boiler by the LNER to enable it to appear in steam at the 1925 Stockton & Darlington Railway centenary celebrations and cavalcade.

It was hardly likely to be scrapped after such an investment, and was assured of a place in the new museum set up by the LNER at York in 1926. At last the engine was on permanent display to the public.

And so it remained, but for only 12 years, as the LNER took it out of the museum and steamed it again in 1938. A 'Flying Scotsman' train of the 1870s

No 1 was brought out of its retirement from the museum York in 1938 to steam again. It was seen on many parts of the LNER system and here is on shed at Norwich in July of that year. COLOUR-RAIL

was assembled with No 1 hauling seven ECJS six-wheelers, as part of the publicity surrounding the LNER's introduction of its new streamlined trains.

No 1 was also hired by the Railway Correspondence & Travel Society, and became the first preserved engine to haul a main line railtour. No 1 quickly returned to the safety of the museum though for WW2 and nationalisation and did not emerge again until it moved to the new National Railway Museum in 1974.

That was all remarkable enough, but in 1981, the NRM returned it to steam for a second time in preservation. The old museum at York had closed in 1974, and the new showpiece National Railway Museum had opened in the old NER roundhouse. The new museum acquired a reputation for steaming engines on special occasions, and No 1 was one of those selected. In fact, just six appearances hauling short trains on the GCR was all the old engine could manage, and even then, No 1's driver from 1938 had to be brought out of retirement, as no-one else could quite master it.

Nevertheless, it was a hugely popular gesture and a real landmark in preservation history which enabled new generations to briefly sample one of Britain's most historic steam engines in action. ∎

No 1 was returned to steam by the National Railway Museum in 1981 and ran for just three weekends on passenger trains on the GCR. The historic engine makes a fine sight as it steams out of Loughborough Central on 8 May 1982.
BRIAN SHARPE.

990 *Henry Oakley*

Above: No longer able to be steamed, and normally on display at Bressingham Steam Museum in Norfolk, No 990 *Henry Oakley* visited Boston for the 150th anniversary of the first railway into the town. On 12 September 1998, the Atlantic is in the company of two other Doncaster-built engines, Class 03 shunter D2112 and EWS Class 56 Type 5 diesel No 56091.
BRIAN SHARPE

Far Right: No 990 *Henry Oakley* was returned to steam at the new National Railway Museum in time to run in the cavalcade from Shildon to Darlington on 31 August 1975.
BRIAN SHARPE

The pioneer GNR Atlantic, built in 1897, was withdrawn from service in 1937. Although quickly succeeded by the 'Large Atlantics', the smaller ones were still kept busy by the LNER up to WWII.

In view of its historic importance, *Henry Oakley* was considered by the LNER to be an ideal candidate for display in its museum at York, which it had established 10 years earlier, largely as a result of having staged the Stockton & Darlington Railway centenary cavalcade.

No 990 was joined after WWII by the first of the 'Large Atlantics', No 251, but neither was destined to be a static exhibit for too long. An entrepreneur enthusiast by the name of Alan Pegler not only had the idea of steaming the two Atlantics again, but he also had the contacts in the railway industry to be

able to make it happen.

The destination for the big railtour was to be none other than 'The Plant' at Doncaster. On 20 September 1953, a trainload of enthusiasts travelled from King's Cross to Doncaster on the 'Plant Centenarian' behind two of Doncaster's most famous products of yesteryear. They visited the works, in its centenary year, and returned to London behind A4 No 60014 *Silver Link*. The Atlantic's drivers on the day were celebrated ECML drivers, Bill Hoole and Ted Hailstone.

Two weeks later, the two veterans repeated the exercise, running from Leeds to King's Cross via Doncaster and Lincoln. The train reached 80mph down Stoke Bank.

No 990 also made an appearance in steam shortly after moving from the old museum at York to the

No 990 *Henry Oakley* departs from Damems Loop on the Keighley & Worth Valley Railway on 11 June 1978. DAVID RODGERS

new one in 1974. It was able to travel under its own steam to Shildon for the Stockton & Darlington 150th anniversary celebrations in August 1975, towing the Stirling Single along the four-track ECML.

The year 1977 saw *Henry Oakley* loaned to the Keighley & Worth Valley Railway to haul passenger trains for the first time since 1953. Unfortunately after a couple of months, it broke down and has never steamed since.

Its failure was just before an appearance at the Railex 125 event at 'The Plant'. It had been booked to double head with *Flying Scotsman* from Keighley to Doncaster, but No 4472 had to tow the Atlantic dead. No 990 returned to the NRM afterwards, but in recent years has been loaned to Bressingham Steam Museum. ∎

No 251

Above: No 251 on display at Bressingham Steam Museum.
BRIAN SHARPE

York's museum provided the impetus for the LNER to preserve a couple more locomotives after it opened in 1926. An obvious choice was the pioneer Ivatt large Atlantic, No 3251, GNR No 251, which was withdrawn from service in 1947.

Returned to original condition at 'The Plant', No 251 went to York to join No 990, the pioneer small Atlantic. There it might have stayed, if it were not for Alan Pegler, who arranged for both Atlantics to leave the museum for a short period of active service.

No 251's active service was a little more extensive than No 990's, for example, working to Liverpool and to Farnborough in 1954. At the time, No 251 was not a particularly old engine, in fact the very last GN Atlantic to be withdrawn from service was No 62822, one of only two to receive a BR number, but which had worked until 1950.

No 251 returned to the museum at York and has never been steamed since. It moved to the new National Railway Museum in 1974, travelled to 'The Plant' at Doncaster for a couple of events, and in 2004 was placed on loan to the Bressingham Steam Museum in Norfolk, reunited with No 990. ∎

Ivatt small Atlantic No 990 *Henry Oakley* and large Atlantic No 251 double head the 'Plant Centenarian' railtour from King's Cross to Doncaster, past Wymondley on 20 September 1953.

Flying Scotsman

Completed just after the Grouping, No 4472 was a GNR-designed engine, originally No 1472. It is probably fair to say that almost from the time of its construction *Flying Scotsman* was one of the most famous steam locomotives in the world, but it reached the end of the line in 1963 at a time when steam engine withdrawal and scrapping was at its height.

The British Transport Commission designated a lot of engines for official preservation, but it could not preserve everything, and a scientific process was used for selection, rather than the fame of the engines.

Gresley had the honour of having two of his locomotive designs selected, the A4 Pacific and the V2 2-6-2. These two told the story of Gresley's most successful locomotive designs quite satisfactorily without the inclusion of an A3. The A3 in any case was nowhere near original, and by 1963 was very different from the A1 that Gresley had first designed in 1922.

It is possible that even if an A3 had been selected for official preservation, and funds allocated for its rebuilding to original condition, *Great Northern* might have been the preferred choice anyway, had it not been extensively rebuilt by Thompson. The first of the class was usually nominated for official preservation, and *Flying Scotsman* was not actually famous enough at that stage to justify an exception as was made in the case of *Mallard* which usurped *Silver Link's* position by virtue of being 14mph faster.

But it was *Flying Scotsman's* withdrawal for scrapping that indirectly led to its world renown in the years ahead.

Purchased by businessman Alan Pegler, restored to LNER apple green livery at 'The Plant' as No 4472 back in single chimney form, and based at Doncaster,

the engine saw intensive use on railtours all over Britain. Alan Pegler had previously been involved in the operation of two preserved GNR Atlantics 10 years earlier.

It was not quite the first privately preserved steam engine to haul main line railtours, but Alan Pegler's position and contacts, as a BR (Eastern Region) board member, enabled him to negotiate a unique contract. *Flying Scotsman* proved able to go where lesser engines could not.

From late 1967 it was the only privately preserved engine allowed to run on BR and from August 1968 the only steam engine of any description to run on BR main lines at all. In 1969 it set off on a tour of North America, which proved financially disastrous, and bankrupted its owner.

Rescued by William (later Sir William) McAlpine, *Flying Scotsman* returned to Britain in 1973 and resumed its railtour operations under very different circumstances, but very successfully until the early 1990s, by which time, it had also undertaken a record-breaking tour of Australia. After some years of uncertainty though, another millionare, Tony Marchington bought it, overhauled it at phenomenal expense and set it to work mainly on up-market luxury dining trains.

Unfortunately, it proved to be his undoing as well, he went bankrupt and the engine was sold, this time to York's National Railway Museum. No 4472 finally became part of the National Collection in 2004, at a cost of £2.31million and 41 years too late.

Currently under heavy overhaul at York, no other steam engine has a history quite like *Flying Scotsman*, both before and after preservation. It will always be the most famous steam locomotive in the world, and it was made in Doncaster. ∎

Above left: *Flying Scotsman* made a brief appearance in its final BR condition as No 60103, though not on main line duties. Recalling the latter days of ECML steam, No 60103 hauls a van train on the Nene Valley Railway on 8 July 1994.
BRIAN SHARPE

Right: While in the ownership of Sir William McAlpine, A3 Pacific No 4472 *Flying Scotsman* departs from Doncaster on 6 March 1983 with the third of a series of railtours on the East Coast Main Line to celebrate the engine's 60th birthday.
BRIAN SHARPE

Flying Scotsman is now undergoing a thorough overhaul at the National Railway Museum. Its last run before withdrawal was a round trip from Birmingham to Trent Junction. Now in double chimney form, complete with German-style smoke deflectors, No 4472 passes Loughborough Midland on 16 December 2005. BRIAN SHARPE

4771 Green Arrow

Gresley's V2 class was singular in that virtually no other 2-6-2 tender engines were ever built in Britain. Despite the number of Pacifics on its books, the LNER built no fewer than 184 of these 2-6-2s, a type not used by any of its contemporaries. Although obviously smaller than the 4-6-2s, the V2s were very nearly their equal, and proved to be one of the most successful classes of engine ever built.

It was the unique wheel arrangement which led to pioneer class member No 4771 *Green Arrow* being selected for official preservation, on its withdrawal from King's Cross shed in 1962. In fact only the first five class members, including No 4771, were built at Doncaster, plus a further 20 later on.

There were no funds available to restore most of the engines being withdrawn for official preservation at that time, unless there was a location earmarked for display, for example in the museum at Clapham or another local museum. In *Green Arrow's* case, a local museum was planned for Doncaster and so No 60800, along with a J17 0-6-0 from Stratford, had a thorough restoration at Doncaster Works, before being put into short-term storage at Hellifield.

The museum proposal never materialised, but another museum was planned later for Leicester. The V2, along with several other officially preserved, but unrestored engines, was selected on the basis that members of the class had worked regularly through Leicester on the ex-GCR route. The museum proposals were curtailed and *Green Arrow* and others went back into storage, this time at Preston Park near Brighton.

A move to Norwich was a surprise development, where one-time shedmaster Bill Harvey oversaw a return to steam. No 4771 proudly steamed from

Norwich to Tyseley in 1974, and took its place among the elite few main line steam engines approved at that time to work on BR main lines.

It was part of the National Collection of course, and when the new National Railway Museum opened at York in 1975, *Green Arrow* was not only assured of a place in the display, but as a firm favourite of museum staff, past and present, has been kept in working order for most of the past 30 years, working hard in all parts

On what will have been its last-ever run into King's Cross, No 4771 speeds through Huntingdon on 18 November 2006. BRIAN SHARPE

of Britain, but rarely leaving York for long.

This looks likely to change though as No 4771 still has the original Gresley design of cylinder block, where all three cylinders and the smokebox saddle are in one casting. This is becoming worn and cannot be repaired, and under the museum's stated policy cannot be replaced either. On expiry of its current boiler certificate in the coming months, *Green Arrow* looks likely to retire from active service for the foreseeable future.

In fact considerable expenditure will be required on the boiler for the engine ever to return to the main line, and No 4771 looks like spending its last few months of active service running at reduced boiler pressure on preserved railways, with a main line return unlikely.

Sadly one of Doncaster's best-known locomotives, which escaped the cutter's torch, may have hauled its last main line train. ■

Always maintained in immaculate condition, the National Railway Museum's LNER V2 2-6-2 No 4771 *Green Arrow* heads north past Bingley Junction, Shipley on 8 September 1990. BRIAN SHARPE

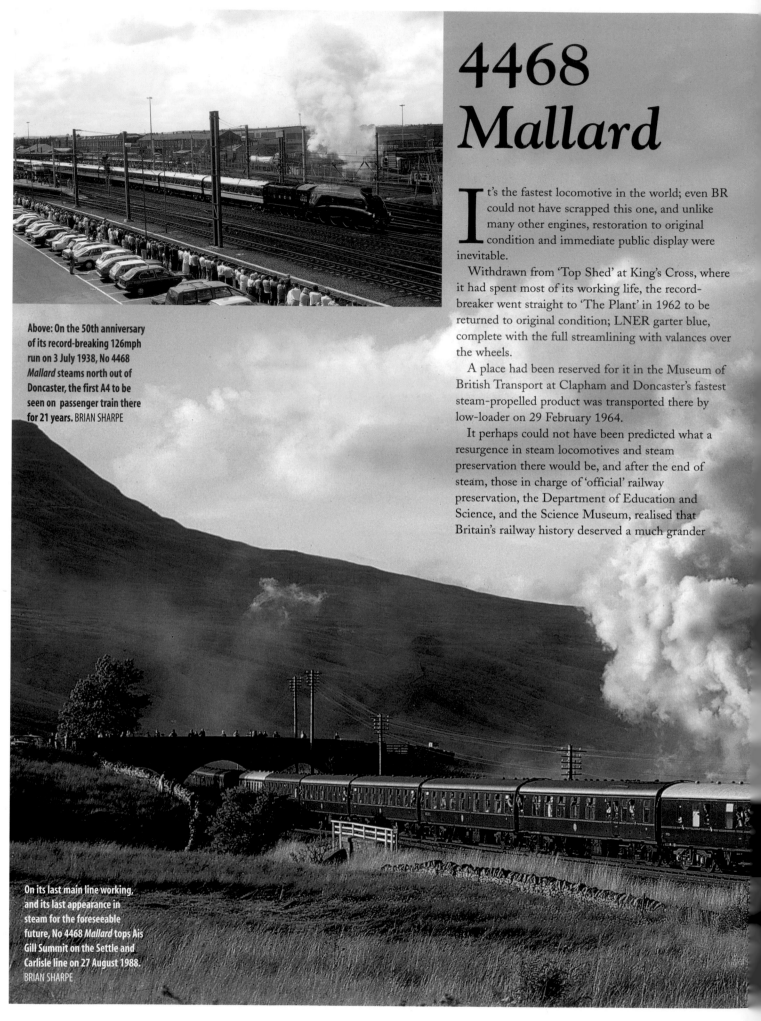

4468 Mallard

I t's the fastest locomotive in the world; even BR could not have scrapped this one, and unlike many other engines, restoration to original condition and immediate public display were inevitable.

Withdrawn from 'Top Shed' at King's Cross, where it had spent most of its working life, the record-breaker went straight to 'The Plant' in 1962 to be returned to original condition; LNER garter blue, complete with the full streamlining with valances over the wheels.

A place had been reserved for it in the Museum of British Transport at Clapham and Doncaster's fastest steam-propelled product was transported there by low-loader on 29 February 1964.

It perhaps could not have been predicted what a resurgence in steam locomotives and steam preservation there would be, and after the end of steam, those in charge of 'official' railway preservation, the Department of Education and Science, and the Science Museum, realised that Britain's railway history deserved a much grander

Above: On the 50th anniversary of its record-breaking 126mph run on 3 July 1938, No 4468 *Mallard* steams north out of Doncaster, the first A4 to be seen on passenger train there for 21 years. BRIAN SHARPE

On its last main line working, and its last appearance in steam for the foreseeable future, No 4468 *Mallard* tops Ais Gill Summit on the Settle and Carlisle line on 27 August 1988. BRIAN SHARPE

Doncaster's Railway Legends

museum. There was also the matter of the huge volume of exhibits, not just locomotives amassed during BR's modernisation, which needed to be displayed. A new National Railway Museum was created at York, opened in 1975, and pride of place went to *Mallard*, built not far away at Doncaster.

Right from the start, the museum appreciated that part of its educational brief should include showing its exhibits in steam occasionally, and planning for *Mallard* to return to steam at least for the 50th anniversary of its 1938 record-breaking run started well before 1988.

Mallard was not in bad condition, having been withdrawn as steam ended, not because it was worn out. However, its boiler ideally needed a major overhaul, which the museum was keen to avoid, as it was not intended to run the engine intensively over a period of several years. A compromise was agreed, only necessary boiler work was carried out and No 4468 was returned to steam in 1986, with a restricted number of steamings permitted over a three-year period.

Mallard journeyed far and wide during its three

years on the main line to Scarborough, Carlisle, Liverpool and London, culminating in a special train commemorating the 50th anniversary of the record run of 3 July 1938.

Surprisingly, No 4468 became the first streamliner to haul a passenger train out of Doncaster for 21 years. It was just before electric services were inaugurated, and the special arrived from King's Cross behind unique Co-Co electric No 89001, the first electrically hauled passenger train to arrive at Doncaster.

A month later though, *Mallard* hauled the final train of the series and returned to its role as a static exhibit at York. ∎

Above: No 4468 *Mallard* prepares to leave York for Manchester on 16 July 1988.
BRIAN SHARPE

4498 *Sir Nigel Gresley*

Sir Nigel Gresley returned to steam after a major overhaul at Grosmont on the North Yorkshire Moors Railway and makes a living hauling trains in *Heartbeat* country. No 60007, in early 1950s BR blue livery, departs from Aidensfield, otherwise known as Goathland on 29 October 2006. BRIAN SHARPE

Back in the 1960s, while *Mallard* was assured of a secure, if static future, *Flying Scotsman* had demonstrated that there was scope for preserved steam engines to carry on working for their living, and a considerable body of enthusiast opinion felt that an active A4 Pacific would be a good idea. A preservation society was formed with the aim of buying one, the one named after its designer being the preferred choice.

Accordingly, when withdrawn 1966, No 60007 was not only bought, but went straight into Crewe Works for a major overhaul, quickly emerging in early 1967 to haul a couple of parcels trains to Preston!

Restored to garter blue livery as No 4498 but without valances, *Gresley* really covered the country on various railtours in the short couple of years before BR introduced its total ban on the operation of privately owned steam engines in late 1967.

After this ban was lifted, No 4498 was one of the first steam engines to return to the main line, with a Newcastle to Carlisle train on 17 June 1972. It has been one of the most widely travelled of all main line preserved engines ever since.

One place that A4s avoided completely for many years though was Doncaster. It just was not permitted, owing to the speed and frequency of trains on the ECML. It was a full seven years after *Mallard's* return to the main line through Doncaster before another A4 was seen hauling a train there, after privatisation had led to a radical shake-up of the rules regarding such operations.

Doncaster's Railway Legends

Sir Nigel Gresley as No 60007 hauled a Newcastle to King's Cross train in June 1995, and in October 1996, called at Doncaster with a King's Cross to Edinburgh train.

Retirement from the main line came in 1999 when No 60007 took up a slightly less arduous existence on the North Yorkshire Moors Railway. A major overhaul was completed in 2006, and the process of upgrading the engine to main line condition is in hand, with a view to No 60007 working main line excursions again in the autumn of 2007. ■

No 4498 shunts its stock at Stratford-upon-Avon on 12 January 1985, before heading to Marylebone; the first steam train to the terminus in the preservation era. The engine was named after its designer in a ceremony at Marylebone in 1937. BRIAN SHARPE

A4 Pacific No 4498 *Sir Nigel Gresley* heads north out of Leeds for Carnforth on 30 April 1977 through Calverley Cutting; its train including a restored Gresley buffet car.
BRIAN SHARPE

60009 *Union of South Africa*

No 60009 was always a Scottish engine. A small number of the class were based at Haymarket shed in Edinburgh, and rarely travelled as far south as even Doncaster, let alone King's Cross, except of course on non-stop workings. LNER policy was for engines to stay at one shed for much of their working lives, and this was perpetuated throughout BR steam days.

Despite this, it was No 60009 that hauled BR's very last steam train out of King's Cross on 24 October 1964, becoming the last A4 to pass through Doncaster in BR passenger service.

Union of South Africa, towards the end of its career, did move, to join the fleet of A4s at Aberdeen, for working the three-hour expresses to Glasgow. It was one of the last to work these trains, but withdrawal came in early 1966, its last duty being haulage of an 18-coach railtour at Easter that year, assisted by an LMS 'Black Five' 4-6-0.

Purchased immediately by John Cameron, farmer and businessman, No 60009 was moved to Lochty, Fife, where the trackbed of a branch line ran across his farm. Mr Cameron relaid some track and ran his engine with an LNER 'Beavertail' observation car on this short length of line, hardly a fitting retirement for a streamlined Pacific.

Once BR started to show a more enlightened attitude to the operation of preserved steam engines, No 60009 moved to the goods shed at nearby Markinch and prepared to recapture its past glories on the Aberdeen road.

It acquired an enthusiastic following, running occasionally on the lines it was associated with, and looking just as it had in BR service. It was not until 1984 that the engine ventured south of the border for the first time in preservation.

From 1994 to 2007, No 60009 was based on the Severn Valley Railway where it saw occasional use, but it has been seen in all parts of Britain, from Plymouth to Waterloo; Holyhead to Inverness.

'Number Nine's real moment of glory though was on 29 October 1994 when it steamed out of King's Cross once again, almost exactly 30 years after that final steam departure in BR service.

The 1994 'Elizabethan' went no further north than Peterborough, but it was groundbreaking in that it established the precedent for operating steam on electrified inter-city main lines.

Even so, while *Sir Nigel Gresley* made occasional appearances in Doncaster, No 60009 remained much rarer, not being seen on a passenger train there until 2005. It has since become a much more familiar sight, but in 2007 moved to a new home in Scotland, at Thornton Junction. ■

Left: No 60009 has often been seen passing through Doncaster in recent years, but does not always arrive from King's Cross. On 16 December 2006, *Union of South Africa* passes the Great Central station at Mexborough with a tour from Mill Hill to York. BRIAN SHARPE

Above: A4 Pacific No 60009 *Union of South Africa* spent its working life based in Scotland, and continued to run exclusively north of the border in preservation for many years. It is seen hauling a railtour through Dalmeny Junction just south of the Forth Bridge on 28 May 1977. In 2007 it returned to Scotland to a new base at Thornton Junction. BRIAN SHARPE

Left: 'Number nine' speeds south on the East Coast Main Line past the Edinburgh 200 miles sign at Benningborough on 19 May 2007, with the Railway Touring Company's 'Hadrian' tour. TREVOR LAW

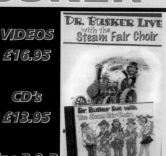

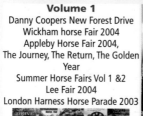

Pacifics across the Atlantic

The story of how one of Gresley's Doncaster-built streamlined A4 Pacifics ended up in the American mid-west state of Wisconsin, was lost in the mists of time until relatively recently.

In the 1950s, as steam was obliterated from US railroads somewhat quicker than in Britain, a National Railroad Museum was established in Green Bay, Wisconsin, by the Great Lakes, west of Chicago. It was a chance conversation between a lady called Mrs Kovachek, who was on holiday from Yorkshire, and a chap she thought was the gardener, that led to the locomotive emigrating to the States. The gardener was in fact the chairman of the museum's board, Harold E Fuller and when he found out that there was a locomotive named *Dwight D Eisenhower* in the UK, he simply had to have it for the collection. BR however would not sell it to him.

The LNER's No 4496 *Golden Shuttle* had been renamed after the US war hero and later President, but in the late 1950s was still hard at work on BR express services. General Eisenhower had strong connections with Britain's railways as there had been two military command trains in Britain during the run-up to D-Day, which were for the general's exclusive use. These trains, mainly of GWR stock and code-named 'Alive' did include two LNER Gresley coaches, which were the general's favourites. When No 60008 was withdrawn, along with several of the King's Cross allocation, in 1963, BR was happy to donate the engine and the two LNER coaches used by General Eisenhower, to the Green Bay museum.

There they were displayed together for many years from 1964.

It is only in recent years that research on both sides of the Atlantic has led its US custodians to realise that *Dwight D Eisenhower* would almost certainly never have hauled either of its namesake's military trains in Britain during WWII.

Still in BR green livery, as restored at 'The Plant' prior to export, the A4 in 2000 has been given pride of place in a new museum building at Green Bay, still with the Gresley coaches attached, and standing alongside Union Pacific 'Big-Boy' articulated 4-8-8-4 No 4017. A member of the world's fastest class of steam engines, stands next to the world's biggest.

The story of how another A4 Pacific also came to cross the Atlantic is perhaps a little less interesting. A National Railroad Museum was also set up in Canada, and with No 60008 already donated for preservation in the USA, BR could hardly refuse a request from the Canadian museum in Montreal for No 60010 *Dominion of Canada*.

No 4489 was one of the early batches of A4s that carried apple green livery and the name *Woodcock*. A batch of A4s received Commonwealth names and garter blue livery, for working the LNER 'Coronation' and 'West Riding Limited' expresses, and No 4489 was renamed *Dominion of Canada* and repainted garter blue within two weeks of entering service, becoming No 60010 in BR days.

No 60010 was withdrawn somewhat later, in 1965, having been one of those transferred to Scotland to work the Aberdeen expresses. It was restored at Crewe works coincidentally at the same time as privately purchased No 60007 *Sir Nigel Gresley*. While *Gresley* acquired garter blue livery, *Dominion of Canada* retained BR green.

It was shipped to Canada in April 1967. Neither of the expatriate A4s has ever been steamed in preservation, and there is little prospect of either returning to Britain. ■

A4 Pacific No 60010 *Dominion of Canada* at Montreal.
PETER CUNNINGHAM

A4 Pacific No 60008 *Dwight D Eisenhower* at the US National Railroad Museum, Green Bay, Wisconsin. WILLIE BATH

60019 *Bittern*

Right: *Bittern's* boiler is lowered into the frames during its overhaul on the Mid-Hants Railway at Ropley. CEDRIC JOHNS

No 60019 was an A4 normally associated with the North Eastern Region, but was one of the select members of the class that moved to Aberdeen for the last couple of years of the Glasgow-Aberdeen expresses. It survived to become one of the last two of the class in BR service, withdrawn in September 1966.

No 60019 ended its career, by hauling BR's last A4-hauled train, from Glasgow to Aberdeen and back on 3 September. Next day, after its sister No 60024 *Kingfisher* hauled a railtour from Edinburgh to Aberdeen, *Bittern* took over the train and hauled it all the way to York, where it entered private preservation in the ownership of Geoffrey Drury. It was just able to make a couple of trips in private ownership before BR's steam ban took effect in 1967.

Restored to LNER garter blue at York as No 19, *Bittern* also made a couple of runs to Scarborough in 1972-73 after the lifting of the steam ban, but then retired completely, in need of heavy repairs.

Geoffrey Drury, who had bought *Bittern*, later also bought A2 Pacific No 60532 *Blue Peter*, and both locomotives were very much later put in the custody of the North Eastern Locomotive Preservation Group.

Bittern was cosmetically restored as pioneer A4 No 2509 *Silver Link* and displayed for several years in this condition. It was later stripped for overhaul on the Great Central Railway at Loughborough, but before any serious restoration took place, it was bought by Tony Marchington, the then-millionaire owner of *Flying Scotsman*.

Mr Marchington's ambitious plans involved the restoration of both locomotives, for use on an intensive programme of luxury dining trains. The plans never came to fruition though and restoration of *Bittern* to running order only really started in January 2001 after purchase by Jeremy Hosking, wealthy owner of a number of main line steam locomotives.

The overhaul has been carried out at the Mid-Hants Railway's base at Ropley and was one of the heaviest overhauls to be carried out on a main line steam locomotive, the locomotive having suffered a cracked frame. The boiler overhaul was carried out at Chatham, and was in itself a major task.

Initially masterminded by Roland Kennington, who had carried out the overhaul of *Flying Scotsman* for Tony Marchington at Southall, No 60019, back in BR Brunswick green livery, finally steamed again in early 2007.

Completion of the work has now seen *Bittern* take

its place among the fleet of working 'streaks', alongside *Sir Nigel Gresley* and *Union of South Africa*.

No 60019 hauled its first passenger train since 1973, on 7 July 2007, on the Mid-Hants Railway from Alton to Alresford, during a gala weekend to celebrate the 40th anniversary of the end of steam on the Southern Region.

Above: *Bittern's* last main line run was as LNER No 19 in garter blue livery from Hull to Scarborough on 21 April 1973, seen near Bridlington. D ROWE
Below: *Bittern* spent many years cosmetically restored as No 2509 *Silver Link*. BRIAN SHARPE

Bittern departs from Alresford with its first public passenger train since restoration. JON POTTER

Its main line debut is eagerly awaited. It was never one of the 'celebrity' A4s in real steam days, except right at the end of its days, in the mid 1960's, on the Aberdeen road, and it has been one of the 'Cinderellas' of steam preservation, out in the wilderness for 34 years.

Indications are though, that its day has finally arrived. Now set for 15 September 2007, *Bittern's* return to the main line should be at the head of a 70th anniversary of the 'Coronation' streamliner, running from King's Cross to Scarborough and return, with a second tender to avoid the necessity for any water stops en route.

When No 60019 passes through Doncaster once again, for the first time since 1964, it could be at the start of a second coming that will see the engine become one of 'The Plant's most celebrated products in its second career in the preservation era. ■

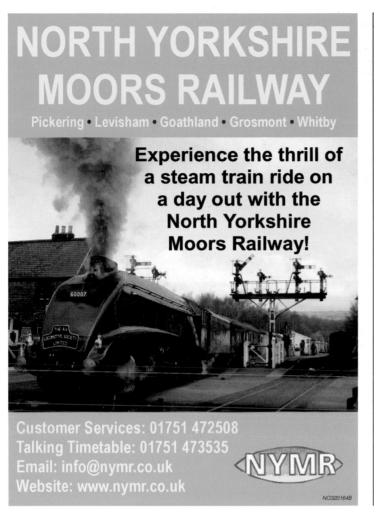
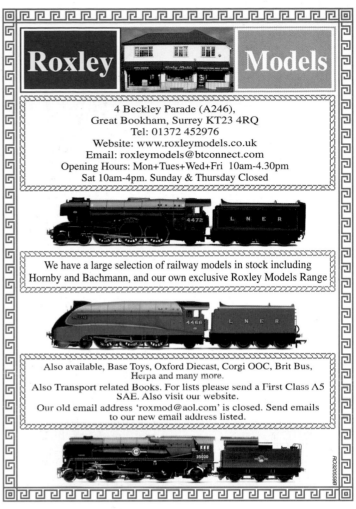

60532 *Blue Peter*

Of the express Pacifics, built by the 'Big Four' after 1923, an example of every class has been preserved, either officially or privately, in some cases in considerable numbers, with one exception.

Designed by Peppercorn, the last CME of the LNER, Blue Peter was completed at Doncaster on 25 March 1948 with a single chimney, in LNER apple green livery but numbered 60532 and lettered 'BRITISH RAILWAYS' on the tender. It was initially allocated to York for working express trains on the ECML. At its first general overhaul it was fitted with a double blastpipe and chimney, together with a multiple valve regulator in the smokebox. It was then allocated to Ferryhill (Aberdeen) to work the heaviest trains between there and Edinburgh.

The LNER Pacifics, nearly all Doncaster-built, were consigned to the scrapyard over quite a short period of time, and only one, the streamlined A4 *Mallard*, was selected for official preservation, as a static museum exhibit. The so-called 'Indian summer' of the A4s in Scotland prolonged the lives of some of the class, and added to their popularity. So, not only did the A4s outlive virtually all of the much newer Pacifics, but private purchasers opted almost exclusively for the streamliners, while the non-streamlined A3, *Flying Scotsman* was the first to be bought, the next three to enter preservation were all A4s. Meanwhile the A1s all went for scrap, and the A2s very nearly did as well.

Fortunately, the last of the A2s, which worked in Scotland until late 1966, No 60532 *Blue Peter*, escaped being scrapped long enough for the owner of A4 No 60019 *Bittern*, Geoff Drury, to buy it too.

Its preserved career has been chequered. Restored at Doncaster to non-authentic LNER apple green as No 532, it took part in a hugely popular open day at Doncaster Works with TV coverage and 60,000 visitors witnessed its renaming by BBC *Blue Peter* TV presenters, but it was not in steam.

It was eventually steamed, ran down to Tyseley in 1974 with a couple of coaches, and back again, then disappeared into storage at Walton Colliery near Wakefield.

Transferred to the Dinting Railway Centre, it was steamed again, and was seen at Didcot in 1985, but after 20 years of preservation was still no nearer to hauling a main line passenger train.

Salvation came in the shape of the North Eastern Locomotive Preservation Group.

Left: On a rare appearance in steam in the 1980s in LNER apple green livery, No 532 *Blue Peter* hauls a short train at the Didcot Railway Centre on 2 June 1985.
BRIAN SHARPE

Right: No 532 *Blue Peter* is rolled out of 'The Plant' on 18 July 1969, prior to its renaming by the Blue Peter TV programme in front of 60,000 people.
MAURICE BURNS COLLECTION

Below: Towards the end of its boiler certificate, No 60532 *Blue Peter* ran on the North Yorkshire Moors Railway between Grosmont and Pickering. The engine is now on static display at Barrow Hill Roundhouse, Staveley.
BRIAN SHARPE

With much assistance from ICI Wilton, where it arrived on 16 December 1986, and with thousands of NELPG volunteer man-hours, it was restored as No 60532 and again renamed by the BBC programme in December 1991. After some running-in on the NYMR that Christmas, it achieved its main line certificate in 1992.

Further running on the main line saw No 60532 pass occasionally through Doncaster, including on an Edinburgh to King's Cross special in May 1998. Sadly, Geoff Drury died on 18 October 1999 but the locomotive remains the property of his family. It is currently in need of a major overhaul but negotiations regarding this are continuing.

Blue Peter has carried the flag alone for post-Gresley Pacific locomotive design at Doncaster, the only Pacific built at Doncaster by British Railways to have survived into preservation. It is theoretically Britain's most powerful Pacific and its performance has proved that claim to have some justification.

Its 6ft 2in wheels give it the extra tractive effort, although speed was clearly not compromised too much. During trials in 1951 between single- and double-chimney A2s, No 60532 achieved 100mph on the 'Aberdonian' between Stonehaven and Montrose. ∎

60163 *Tornado*

Doncaster built two series of Pacifics which were classified as A1s. First came Gresleys in 1922, starting with *Great Northern, Sir Frederick Banbury* and *Flying Scotsman*. Much later, from 1948 came Peppercorn's A1s, which were a much more modern design, and should have become the premier express steam locomotives on the East Coast Main Line.

There was nothing wrong with them, they were much more economical, particularly in maintenance costs than Gresley's Pacifics, but they were inclined to be rough-riding and the crews never took to them as well as the A3s and A4s.

Sadly none of Peppercorn's 6ft 8in Pacifics, the A1s escaped the scrapman. The last of the class No 60145 *St Mungo*, withdrawn from York shed in April 1966, was quickly scrapped at Hull, leaving a very significant gap in British express steam locomotive preservation.

At a press launch in York in 1990, it was announced that the A1 Steam Locomotive Trust was going to build a new Peppercorn A1 Pacific. The idea was that individual covenantors would take out a monthly subscription, giving a guaranteed annual income to the Trust, which, with sponsorship and other assistance from business, would enable the locomotive to be constructed within an acceptable timescale. The actual cost per week to each individual covenantor could be minimal and it was billed as building 'an A1 for the price of a pint'.

The Trust is now close to completing Britain's newest express steam engine, to Peppercorn's Doncaster design of 1947. Twenty-six of the original class were built at Doncaster, and 23 at Darlington, the new one, not a replica, but an entirely new engine,

The frame assembly for *Tornado* at Darlington in 1999, with cylinders and cab fitted. PETE KELLY

Left: Dorothy Mather, widow of A1 designer, Arthur Peppercorn, with the engine's new boiler. A1 STEAM LOCOMOTIVE TRUST

incorporating major enhancements to the original specification, is being assembled at Darlington.

The first job was to scan the original drawings from the Doncaster design office, a huge task in itself, but accomplished by an army of volunteers with assistance from the National Railway Museum. The frames were actually erected at Tyseley Locomotive Works in Birmingham in January 1995, when No 60163 came into existence.

On 29 September 1997, the original 1853 Stockton & Darlington Railway carriage works building in Darlington, to be used for the assembly of the locomotive, was opened by Dorothy Mather, widow of the late Arthur Peppercorn. This workshop was funded by Darlington Borough Council, National Heritage Memorial Fund and European Regional Development Fund.

The name adopted for the new engine was *Tornado*, not a racehorse name, but after an aircraft that became famous during the Gulf War. It has proved an appropriate name, and everyone recognises *Tornado* as being the new A1 Pacific.

Most major parts, including wheels and cylinders, have been manufactured and fitted to the frames, and in July 2006 anew completed boiler, the most expensive single item, arrived from Meiningen works in Germany. On 27 June 2007, the boiler was lowered onto the frames. *Tornado* now looks like a complete engine, and the year 2007, should see No 60163 in steam.

The story of the heyday of Doncaster's steam legends is far from over. A whole new, exciting chapter will be opened up over the next few months by No 60163 *Tornado*, the world's first new express steam locomotive to be built for at least 35 years. ■

Privatisation of British Railways

Doncaster was the meeting point of the GNR and the NER, then it was all LNER; later under BR, it was the meeting point of the ER and NER. In 2007, all the ECML expresses are run by Great North Eastern Railways.

British Railways in 1948 was subdivided into six regions, but the Eastern and North Eastern regions merged in 1966. While this regional structure continued right through to privatisation in 1994, train operation became increasingly separated from track and infrastructure. Trains through Doncaster in later BR days, were run by Inter-City (expresses), Railfreight, Regional Railways and Rail Express Systems (parcels and mail).

Railfreight was then divided into three; Mainline, Transrail and Loadhaul.

Privatisation saw track and infrastructure transferred to Railtrack, while train operations were sold piecemeal to various Train Operating Companies (TOCs). The Eastern Region was no more, and Railtrack divided itself into broadly similar zones.

GNER was the TOC that took on the East Coast Main Line franchise, and the Inter-City liveried Class 91 + Mk4 sets, and HSTs acquired the familiar dark blue with vermillion stripe livery.

Meanwhile, the entire freight operation was bought by Ed Burckhart's American-owned English Welsh & Scottish Railways (EWS). This buy-out incorporated the parcels and mail trains, as well as special passenger trains, including the Royal Train.

EWS established its headquarters at Doncaster, giving the town a continuing vital role in the brave new world of the privatised railway system.

The variety of train liveries to be seen passing through Doncaster has continued to grow, and the town even had the last laugh on George Hudson's York & North Midland Railway route to the north, when Richard Branson's Virgin Trains services started to run from Sheffield to York via Doncaster.

After a very promising start, EWS has seen some reversal in its fortunes, as new freight operators have been established, and Freightliner Heavy Haul in particular has made serious inroads into the coal-

Above: Freightliner Class 66/5 No 66578 heads a northbound freightliner train away from Doncaster. BRIAN SHARPE

Above left: An up GNER express passes Decoy yard. A Freightliner Class 66/5 and two EWS Class 67s including silver No 67029 wait in the yard. BRIAN SHARPE

Right: EWS Class 60 No 60078 still carrying main line blue livery brings a freightliner train from Humberside into Doncaster. BRIAN SHARPE

haulage business. EWS also lost the Royal Mail contract, as this traditional railway business moved entirely to road and air transport. Doncaster's relatively new Royal Mail terminal at Potteric Carr Junction closed.

Railtrack of course is no more, superseded by Network Rail. One of EWS's first moves was to purchase diesel locomotives from the US builder General Motors. This virtually sounded the death knell for the British locomotive building industry, and even heavy maintenance of main line locomotives is often no longer carried out at the traditional locomotive workshops.

In 2007, the ECML franchise is up for imminent renewal, and GNER's parent company, Sea Containers is in difficulty. It is likely that a new company will be running ECML trains soon, carrying a totally new livery. No doubt the company will seek to improve still further on the speed and service of ECML expresses, in the tradition of Stirling, Ivatt and Gresley, and later continued by Inter-City and GNER. ■

Privatisation of 'The Plant'

'The Plant' has seen threats to its existence in recent years. First, the contraction of the railway system, and changeover from steam to diesel and electric traction, reduced the volume of locomotive building, overhaul and heavy repair work.

In 1968, a major reorganisation saw the creation of British Rail Engineering Ltd (BREL), a subsidiary of BR, with 13 major works including Doncaster. The new company was able to tender for work outside BR.

As other works closed, Doncaster took on a greater role in wagon work. In 1986-87, BREL was split into two, each part had just four workshops each, four for maintenance and four for construction and heavy repair; Doncaster was not to be in either.

A National Supply Centre (NSC) was to be established and BREL management at Doncaster put forward a proposal, which was accepted, and a part of 'The Plant' took on this role, ensuring a continuation of railway work at the site. Major parts of the plant also continued as a British Rail Maintenance Ltd (BRML), 'Level 5' maintenance depot, continuing to handle heavy locomotive work. Closure of 'The Plant' was averted.

RFS Industries bought the remainder of 'The Plant' in a management buy-out in October 1987. BR retained the offices, but rented the original GNR part to RFS. Despite expanding its customer base, the economic climate was wrong as privatisation was imminent, and RFS went into receivership in 1993.

The NSC became Railpart (UK) Ltd, then was

sold to the Unipart Group, widening its scope for railway work, including train maintenance contracts.

Even before privatisation of the railway system itself, the workshops were increasingly becoming separate business units, owned by outside investors, and competing for work outside of BR. 'The Plant' needed to adapt to rapidly changing circumstances.

The BRML Level 5 depot continued to function and in June 1995, it was privatised, being sold to Asea Brown Boveri (ABB). Its workload increased with the closure of ABB's carriage works at York.

In 1996, ABB merged with Daimler-Benz to become Adtranz. In 2001 Adtranz was acquired by Bombardier Transportation.

RFS continued to trade in receivership and eventually a substantial part of the business was sold to Bombardier ProRail, but the work and much of the equipment was moved to the company's site at Horbury in West Yorkshire.

The residual business and assets were acquired by former middle management who used the name RFS(E). Having built up the business, this in turn was sold to WABCO in 1998 (Westinghouse Air Brake Company), now known as Wabtec Corporation after an American merger, the former RFS(E) now being Wabtec Rail Ltd.

Privatisation has succeeded in attracting outside investment, and some of this has gone into establishing new maintenance facilities on green-field sites, rather than at the traditional railway workshops. Many locomotive workshops have closed; the GWR's Swindon works is no more, and the SR's Eastleigh works in Hampshire has recently also closed.

'The Plant' at Doncaster has proved to be able to adapt itself to the requirements of the modernised, privatised railway industry. It may not build express locomotives, or handle heavy repairs on main line locomotives any more, but the various business units still carry out vital work on a variety of projects to help keep the trains running. ∎

An EWS Class 67 in front of Denison House, the earliest part of 'The Plant'. EWS has its headquarters in Doncaster.
BRIAN SHARPE

'The Plants' other locomotives

The Northern Ireland Railways' 101 Class consisted of the three diesels designed for use hauling the 'Enterprise' passenger services between Belfast and Dublin. All three were named, using names previously carried by the Great Northern Railway (Ireland) Class V locomotives. No 102 *Falcon*, which was withdrawn in 1998, is seen at the Railway Preservation Society of Ireland site at Whitehead, where No 101 is also stored. PAUL BASON

In the good old days, the main line railway workshops built engines for their own main line use, while private contractors built engines for main line use, industrial service or export. Eventually that distinction became more blurred.

It was the diversification into diesel traction that led to major changes, as the private contractors led the way, building diesels for export, and smaller ones for industrial service, and were already well established in the new lines of business when the BR workshops eventually started to produce main line diesels.

The formation of BREL was seen as a way of creating a level playing field so that the main line workshops could compete for business in markets they had not traditionally been involved in. As the number of such workshops declined, so the surviving ones, such as Doncaster tried hard to pick up additional business to keep the order books full as the BR main line work was contracting.

An early example of 'The Plant' getting involved in locomotive building for export was the construction of three 1350hp Bo-Bo diesels for Northern Ireland Railways in 1969. This would have been undreamed of in the heyday of Doncaster Works of course, but it was a sign of changing times. Remarkably, these three engines were extremely significant in that they were

'The Plants' first-ever main line diesels. Yet they were not an example of a BREL works being successful in attracting orders for outside work against competition from the private locomotive builders. It was simply a case of the Hunslet Engine Company having such full order books that it did not have the capacity to construct the engines and subcontracted parts of the job to BREL at Doncaster.

However, it was at least an example of a traditional railway workshop diversifying to survive, and it has proved to be a very rare example. BREL's Class 58 heavy freight diesel, built at Doncaster was seen to have export potential, but it never happened, at least not when they were new, although some redundant ones have been to France recently.

Doncaster also built battery electric locomotives for London Transport in 1973-74.

Only one more large, tangible, locomotive product emerged from Doncaster in the brave new world of privatisation and free competition for non-traditional markets. A huge industrial Co-Co shunter was built in 1993-94 by RFS Industries, for the Tilcon limestone quarry at Swinden in the Yorkshire Dales. Now named *Cracoe*, it still shunts the heavy trains of limestone for Tarmac Ltd, the present quarry owners, one of the last Doncaster-built locomotives in commercial service. ∎

Doncaster Plant 150

The LNER D49 4-4-0s were designed by Gresley, but all built at Darlington. Nevertheless, the one surviving example, No 246 *Morayshire* made the long journey by road from the Bo'ness & Kinneil Railway in Central Scotland to be part of the display at Doncaster. BRIAN SHARPE

The anniversaries of the opening of 'The Plant' at Doncaster in 1853, have been celebrated by what appear to have been ever-bigger events. The 125th anniversary in 1978 was in BR days, and the exhibition staged consisted mainly of Doncaster-built steam engines provided by the nearby National Railway Museum at York.

By 2003, profound changes had taken place at the site, with it having been broken up into several privately owned sections. One of the main private operators of a substantial part of the site, Wabtec Rail, took on the responsibility of staging an impressive display of steam, modern traction and coaching stock, mostly with Doncaster connections, for the 150th anniversary.

More than 30,000 visitors took advantage of sunshine and soaring temperatures to revel in 150 years of Doncaster Works history, myth and legend as Wabtec Rail threw open its doors to the public on 26-27 July.

Doncaster's Railway Legends

Opposite: LNER Pacifics, A3 No 4472 *Flying Scotsman*, and A4s Nos 4468 *Mallard* and 60009 *Union of South Africa.* MAURICE BURNS

Right: LNER V2 2-6-2 No 60800 *Green Arrow*, D49 4-4-0 No 246 *Morayshire* and B1 4-6-0 No 1306 *Mayflower.* MAURICE BURNS

Below: A3 Pacific No 4472 *Flying Scotsman* was repainted in its familiar LNER apple green livery by Wabtec Ltd ready for its appearance at the event. In the background is A4 Pacific No 60009 *Union of South Africa.* BRIAN SHARPE

It was certainly hard to remember a bigger and better gathering of LNER locomotives and stock since the demise of BR steam 35 years ago. From the National Railway Museum came V2 2-6-2 No 60800 *Green Arrow*, GNR Stirling Single No 1 and 4-4-2 No 251 and A4 Pacific No 4468

Mallard, the world's fastest steam engine.

Also on display from the National Collection were GNR 4-4-2 No 990 *Henry Oakley*, GCR O4 2-8-0 No 63601 and GNR J52 0-6-0ST No 68846.

Then there was D49 4-4-0 No 246 *Morayshire* on static display, assembled by Scottish Railway

The National Railway Museum's pioneer Stirling Single 4-2-2 No 1.
BRIAN SHARPE

Preservation Society engineers in a marathon round-the-clock effort to get it ready for the big event, even though its overhaul was not yet completed, B1 4-6-0 No 1306 *Mayflower* from the Nene Valley Railway, A4 No 60009 *Union of South Africa* from the Severn Valley Railway and A3 Pacific No 4472 *Flying Scotsman*, which was reunited with Alan Pegler, the man who bought it from BR in 1963, and NER J21 0-6-0 No 65033 from Beamish Museum.

But many visitors said that despite the magnificent display of locomotives, what really stole the show for them was the matching GNR and LNER teak coaches that had been gathered together to stand behind them. Such vehicles included the Bluebell Railway's GNR director's saloon, the Vintage

Carriages Trust's GNR composite brake No 2856, two maroon-liveried TPO vehicles from Railway Vehicle Preservations on the Great Central Railway and Stephen Middleton's East Coast Joint Stock coach No 189.

Modern traction fans also had much to celebrate, with the superbly arranged display of ancient and modern side by side, including the NRM's Class 71 E5001, Barrow Hill-based Class 83 E3035, Deltic Preservation Society duo D9009 *Alycidon* and No 55019 *Royal Highland Fusilier*, and Howard Johnston's Fragonset-liveried 1959-built Class 31 No 31106 *Spalding Town*, said to be the oldest BR locomotive running in regular main line service, as well as guest engines from EWS, Freightliner,

The pioneer Doncaster-built Class 58 diesel No 58001, restored to original condition by EWS.
ROBIN JONES

Above: Doncaster-built Class 85 electric No 85101, which was named *Doncaster Plant 150 1853-2003* **at the event.** ROBIN JONES

Above right: Doncaster-built Class 71 SR electric E5001 and WCML AL1 Bo-Bo E3035. ROBIN JONES

Cotswold Rail, GB Railfreight and DRS.

The AC Locomotive Group's sole surviving Class 85, Doncaster, 1961-built No 85101 was named *Doncaster Plant 150 1853-2003* on the Sunday, when a Veterans' Day reunion of more than 200 former Doncaster Works workers whose employment stretched as far back as 1926, were given a guided tour. The locomotive was named by railway authors Peter Townend and Dick Hardy, both former Plant employees, accompanied by Wabtec engineering director Mike Roe and Humphrey Gillott of the Railway Mission Chaplaincy.

Virtually all of the exhibits had been either designed, built, shedded or overhauled at Doncaster.

There was also widespread praise for Mike Roe, who had pulled out all the stops to complete the

stunning line-ups. Mike commented: "We were delighted with it – it exceeded our greatest expectations. As well as amassing so many Doncaster engines together, we managed to remind people that until 1965 it was also a major centre for coachbuilding."

The main beneficiary of profits from the open weekend was the Yorkshire-based Bluebell Wood Children's Hospice Appeal, whose representative, Peter Bramley, performed the naming ceremony for Fragonset Class 47 No. 47715 *Poseidon*. ∎

GNR Stirling Single No 1 and A4 No 60009 *Union of South Africa*. MAURICE BURNS